1,000,000 Books

are available to read at

Forgotten Books

www.ForgottenBooks.com

Read online
Download PDF
Purchase in print

ISBN 978-1-331-61599-6
PIBN 10213328

This book is a reproduction of an important historical work. Forgotten Books uses
state-of-the-art technology to digitally reconstruct the work, preserving the original format
whilst repairing imperfections present in the aged copy. In rare cases, an imperfection in
the original, such as a blemish or missing page, may be replicated in our edition. We do,
however, repair the vast majority of imperfections successfully; any imperfections that
remain are intentionally left to preserve the state of such historical works.

Forgotten Books is a registered trademark of FB &c Ltd.
Copyright © 2018 FB &c Ltd.
FB &c Ltd, Dalton House, 60 Windsor Avenue, London, SW19 2RR.
Company number 08720141. Registered in England and Wales.

For support please visit www.forgottenbooks.com

1 MONTH OF FREE READING

at

www.ForgottenBooks.com

By purchasing this book you are eligible for one month membership to ForgottenBooks.com, giving you unlimited access to our entire collection of over 1,000,000 titles via our web site and mobile apps.

To claim your free month visit:
www.forgottenbooks.com/free213328

* Offer is valid for 45 days from date of purchase. Terms and conditions apply.

English
Français
Deutsche
Italiano
Español
Português

www.forgottenbooks.com

Mythology Photography **Fiction** Fishing Christianity **Art** Cooking Essays Buddhism Freemasonry Medicine **Biology** Music **Ancient Egypt** Evolution Carpentry Physics Dance Geology **Mathematics** Fitness Shakespeare **Folklore** Yoga Marketing **Confidence** Immortality Biographies Poetry **Psychology** Witchcraft Electronics Chemistry History **Law** Accounting **Philosophy** Anthropology Alchemy Drama Quantum Mechanics Atheism Sexual Health **Ancient History Entrepreneurship** Languages Sport Paleontology Needlework Islam **Metaphysics** Investment Archaeology Parenting Statistics Criminology **Motivational**

THE LIFE OF EDWARD FITZ-GERALD

BY JOHN GLYDE

With an Introduction by EDWARD CLODD
Sometime President of the Omar Khayyám Club

C. ARTHUR PEARSON, LTD.
HENRIETTA STREET, W.C.
LONDON: 1900

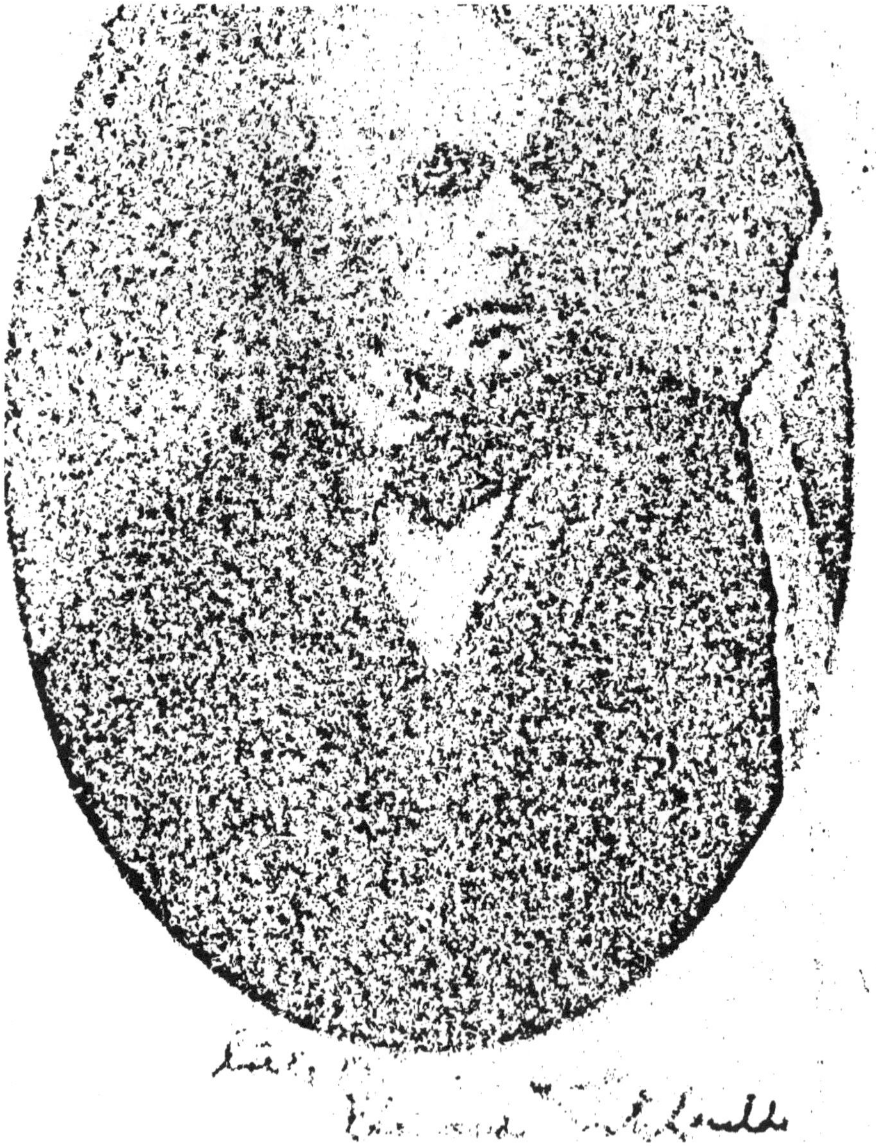

THE LIFE OF
EDWARD FITZ-GERALD
BY JOHN GLYDE

With an Introduction by EDWARD CLODD
Sometime President of the Omar Khayyám Club

C. ARTHUR PEARSON, LTD.
HENRIETTA STREET, W.C.
LONDON: 1900

PR
4703
G58

TO ALL LOVERS OF

EDWARD FITZ-GERALD

ON BOTH SIDES OF THE ATLANTIC

THIS BIOGRAPHY

OF A MAN OF GENIUS

IS RESPECTFULLY INSCRIBED

PREFACE

Hitherto there has been no detailed account of the Life of Edward Fitz-Gerald. The sketch prefixed to the three-volume edition of his *Letters and Literary Remains*, and the articles in *Dictionary of National Biography* and *Chambers's Cyclopædia* are, as may be supposed from their extent, mere skeletons. Fitz-Gerald, by his translation of Omar Khayyám, has been the means of influencing a large number of cultured men and women in England and America. It is natural that such persons should wish to know something of the life and character of the man whose genius they admire, and the formation of the 'Omar Khayyám Club' increased and intensified this desire, to the gratification of which they are legitimately entitled, as the publication of his entire works made him, in the literary world,

Preface

as prominent a character as Shelley or Byron.

The greater portion of the information contained in this Life has been obtained from private sources, from men and women who knew him well, who could describe his habits, who were as familiar with his generosity as with his eccentricity, who knew how tenderly he was beloved by his intimate friends, how sensitive he was to their sufferings, and how deeply he felt their loss.

Among others who have favoured me with anecdotes and recollections of Fitz-Gerald, and to whom I tender my sincere thanks, are Miss Crabbe, Miss Allen, Miss Purcell, Miss Laurence, Mrs. Henry Fawcett, Rev. R. M. Rouse, Rev. C. B. Ratcliffe, Captain Woolner, Mr. Mowbray Donne, Mr. Bernard Quaritch, and Mr. Fox, who as a lad was his 'reader' for a period of three years. To many others I am equally indebted, whose aid has been especially useful, but whose names, in obedience to injunction, I reluctantly with-

Preface

hold. To Mr. Edward Clodd I desire to express my acknowledgment, not only for facts and suggestions, but also for perusing such portion of my Memoir as deals with Fitz-Gerald's translation of *Omar*, and for permission to make use of his privately printed *Pilgrimage to Fitz-Gerald's Grave*.

My thanks also are due, for permission to make extracts from their works, to Lord Tennyson (*Life of the Poet Laureate*); Sir Wemyss Reid (*Life of Lord Houghton*); Macmillan & Co. (*Sir Frederick Pollock's Personal Remembrances*); Bentley & Son (*Fitz-Gerald's Letters to Fanny Kemble*); and to Sampson Low & Co. (*Life and Letters of Charles Samuel Keene*). To the articles on Fitz-Gerald and his works which appeared in the *Quarterly*, the *Edinburgh*, and the *Fortnightly Reviews* I am indebted for hints and suggestions.

February 1, 1900.

INTRODUCTORY NOTE

THE author of this Life has not only spent his life among books, but has added to their number in treatises of value for knowledge of the history of his native country. His narrative of the life of one of its worthies is a fit supplement to these. Mr. Glyde has good warrant for his assumption that a considerable number of readers on both sides of the Atlantic will welcome a somewhat full account of the eccentric recluse, who, in 'mashing together' the quatrains of Omar Khayyám, and transmitting them into noble and stately English verse, unwittingly gave rise to a cult increasing year by year in the number of its votaries, and gained for himself a renown as immortal as it was unsought and undesired.

The horror of publicity which characterised Edward Fitz-Gerald may be advanced in plea for the reticence observed by his

Introductory Note

literary executor, Mr. W. Aldis Wright, when editing the *Letters and Remains*, in dealing with the incidents of a life which ran, with rare interruptions, an even course from childhood to the grave. It is true that we get a well-nigh sufficing portrait of the man in the *Letters*. They evidence that his friendships were, as he says, 'like loves.' Their assessment of literature, both of his own and former times, accord him a place among acute, competent, and incorruptible judges. They assure him a place in the rare company of great letter-writers. Nevertheless, and with all due praise for the restraint which Mr. Aldis Wright has imposed upon himself, the publication of the *Letters* (which Fitz-Gerald never contemplated) being decided upon, the thread of narrative on which they are strung is too thin. For some of them have references, more or less cryptic, to matters upon which explanation is necessary. If the editor's intention was to baulk public curiosity about subjects with which outsiders have no concern (an intention not to be too

Introductory Note

highly commended), the remedy was at hand in the exclusion of letters whose perusal, unhelped by explanation, could only bewilder or tantalise the reader, and give rise to all kinds of surmises.

Mr. Aldis Wright's omissions, however, afford Mr. Glyde his opportunity, and of this he has made tactful and sober use. His materials have been collected with industry and persistence from authentic sources, happily, among these, from the few survivors who knew Fitz-Gerald in the flesh. And although, in the judgment of some, there may be an overlaying of detail, which is no help to the general presentment of the man's characteristics, the broad result is to depict him faithfully—'wrinkles, warts, and all'—in his several relations of husband, friend, and citizen. His place in literature is secure; there is no need to dwell upon that.

It is matter of regret that there should be need to introduce the subject; but the lying legends about Fitz-Gerald's marriage retain such vitality, even in circles where their admission is not suspected, that Mr. Glyde

Introductory Note

has rendered good service in clearing the air of them. The most current one is, that in obedience to the request of his dying friend, Bernard Barton, to 'look after' his daughter Lucy, Fitz-Gerald married her immediately after her father's death, and left her at the church door! Despite references in the *Letters* to the presence of Fitz-Gerald's wife with him in London some months after their marriage, the legend lives on; now, it is to be hoped, receiving its quietus from Mr. Glyde. A more agreeable topic, to which Mr. Glyde refers, is the attitude of Edward Fitz-Gerald (who, if he may be classed at all, is to be classed as an Agnostic) towards the religion of his country as by law established. Replying to a letter from Carlyle, commenting on the 'substantial goodness' found among the villagers, 'resulting from the funded virtues of many good humble men gone by,' Fitz-Gerald says: 'If the old Creed was so commendably effective in the generals and counsellors of two hundred years ago, I think we may be well content to let it work still among the

Introductory Note

ploughmen and weavers of to-day; and even to suffer some absurdities in the form, if the spirit does well on the whole. Even poor Exeter Hall ought, I think, to be borne with' (*Letters*, i. 227, 1894 edition). Three clergymen, Archdeacon Allen, Archdeacon Groome, and the Reverend George Crabbe, were among Fitz-Gerald's closest friends. Probably they never discussed theology with him. His sincerity, manliness, and worth drew out what was best, what was most human, in both cleric and layman; and, for his part, he was wisely content to recognise that a machinery which has, on the whole, worked for the betterment of men, should not be suffered to get out of gear because the pattern is obsolete. The reader may now, without further arrest on my part, pass to a presentment of Edward Fitz-Gerald which, if that be possible, can only enhance his estimation of one of the most striking figures in the great company of high-souled, loveable, and cultivated men.

EDWARD CLODD.

CONTENTS

	PAGE
BIRTH, CHILDHOOD, SCHOOL, AND COLLEGE DAYS	1
FITZ-GERALD BECOMES A HOUSEKEEPER	45
PERSONAL CHARACTERISTICS	83
HIS LITERARY WORK	112
HIS SPANISH AND PERSIAN TRANSLATIONS	141
HIS LIBRARY AND HIS CRITICISMS	187
CARLYLE'S VISIT TO FITZ-GERALD AT WOODBRIDGE	216
MARRIAGE OF EDWARD FITZ-GERALD AND LUCY BARTON	237
LORD HOUGHTON AND LITTLE GRANGE	252
VISITS OF FRIENDS, OLD AND NEW	268

Contents

	PAGE
ALFRED TENNYSON AT WOODBRIDGE .	268
FITZ-GERALD'S LAST DAYS	301

APPENDIX

OFFICIAL COPY OF EDWARD FITZ-GERALD'S WILL	324
LETTER FROM MRS. EDWARD FITZ-GERALD .	338
CERTIFICATE OF MARRIAGE .	340
BIBLIOGRAPHY .	341
INDEX .	353

BIRTH, CHILDHOOD, SCHOOL AND COLLEGE DAYS

THE biography of Edward Fitz-Gerald is the life story of a man who has during the last few years been awarded a niche in the Temple of Fame; though when he died, he was in the literary world known only to a chosen few, and outside his own circle was spoken of as one of the 'casuals of literature.' He was, nevertheless, the valued friend of Alfred Tennyson, Thomas Carlyle, William Makepeace Thackeray, Dr. W. H. Thompson, Master of Trinity College, Cambridge, Professor Cowell, and others. Strange as it may seem, he spent nearly the whole of his life in the little town of Woodbridge, Suffolk, and its immediate neighbourhood; and many of those who lived beside him

The Life of

and knew him well, looked upon him as a benevolent eccentric, strolling through life in Bohemian fashion, regardless of time or money, whilst others (according to his friend Charles Keene, who stayed with him at Woodbridge on three or four occasions) considered him as rather daft!

One of his dearest friends has said that a life like that of Fitz-Gerald has no story. I hope that my readers will feel, before they close this volume, that it is a life worth sketching, and one that conveys lessons of value to students of human nature. At any rate, I know that many persons desire to have a better acquaintance with the man and his career than can at present be obtained. In furnishing this contribution, I hope to be able to remove some misconceptions that are afloat respecting one who, by his inimitable translation, has done more than any other man to make known to English readers the poems of Omar Khayyám, a Persian astronomer, mystic,

Edward Fitz-Gerald

and philosopher of the eleventh century, who has thus become an object of reverential regard in the realms of modern literature.

Edward Fitz-Gerald was born at Bredfield, a small Suffolk village two miles from Woodbridge, on the 31st of March 1809. He was the third son of Mr. John Purcell, who at the time of Edward's birth resided at Bredfield House, an old mansion standing in a well-wooded park, and commanding a fine view of the surrounding country. The district is not rich in scenery, but from the road in front of the lawn people could catch a glimpse of the topmasts of men-of-war lying in Hollesley Bay. Fitz-Gerald liked the idea of the old English manor-house, holding up its inquiring chimneys and weathercocks, which might be espied across fields and pastures from the restless sea. That the surroundings of his home and its immediate neighbourhood made a deep impression upon him is evident from

The Life of

his poem on 'Bredfield House,' in which, when he was thirty years of age, he lovingly described his birthplace, and which is quoted in full further on.

Mr. Purcell was the owner of considerable property, which was largely increased both in Ireland and in Suffolk by his marriage with his cousin Mary Frances Fitz-Gerald, an Irish heiress, who had in addition considerable personal attractions. Upon the death of her father in 1818 he took the name and arms of his wife's family. Mr. Purcell, who thus became Mr. Fitz-Gerald, was an Irish gentleman of social and agreeable disposition, much esteemed in private life, but of no brilliant parts. He amused himself in the ordinary jog-trot fashion of a country gentleman, sharing with Squire Jenny of Hasketon the cost of keeping a pack of harriers, and feeling himself honoured by being selected as High Sheriff of the county, and having a seat in the last unreformed Parliament for the Cinque

Edward Fitz-Gerald

Ports, a constituency which would be classed with pocket boroughs.

We hear it sometimes said that talent comes on the mother's side. It is evident that Edward Fitz-Gerald did not inherit his ability from his father, though it must be admitted that his disposition was in many respects very different from that of his mother. She is said by one of her friends to have been a fine, handsome, clever, and eccentric woman, who in her London home was very fond of display in all her surroundings. That she was wanting in that parental love which warms a woman's heart at the sight of her children would appear from her son's statement, that when he was a child his mother sometimes came up to the nursery, 'but we children were not much comforted by her visit.' No special gifts on the part of the mother are needed to make her children love her, and that such a sensitive child as Edward should thus feel her treatment in the nursery shows that she was deficient in tenderness and sympathy, and that the children had no assurance of her motherly love.

A reviewer who knew Fitz-Gerald well says that 'the chief recollection he seems to have retained of his childhood was the rather terrible, if very splendid, figure of his mother, a great lady who seems to have had a great lady's temper.'

That Edward himself was not wanting in tenderness is shown by the way in which he spoke of his old friend Major Moor, who used to take him by the hand when he was a small boy and lead him to church. Again, how anxiously he wrote inquiring about another favourite of his childhood— Squire Jenny — when the old gentleman was breaking up! The delight he experienced, as a child in the nursery, at seeing the hounds come across the lawn, with his father and Mr. Jenny in their hunting-caps and whips, often recurred to him in middle age.

Edward Fitz-Gerald

After the family went to live at Boulge Hall, his mother astonished the neighbourhood by driving about the country in a coach with four black horses. She was extremely fond of theatrical amusements, was on the most intimate terms with Mrs. Charles Kemble, had a town house in Portland Place, where she invariably resided in the London season, and retained a box at the Haymarket Theatre. Fitz-Gerald said that he had always heard that gout exempted one from many other miseries to which flesh was heir, and he illustrated this by stating that his mother suffered greatly from gout, and was kept awake at night by the pain; but as her head was not affected, her reflections and recollections made the night pass away agreeably.

Young Edward was initiated into French life and manners at an early age. When he was nine years old his father took his family to reside in France. They lived a short time at St. Germains, and after-

The Life of

wards removed to Paris. Few facts of his childhood and boyhood can be obtained, and nothing is known of the educational influences that were at work whilst he sojourned there. The editor of Fitz-Gerald's *Letters*, however, has thrown a side-light on the character of the boy by printing an extract from a letter written by his father to friends in England, in which he tells them that little Edward was full of fun, and fond of making droll speeches, early indications of the humour which characterised his later days. French life and manners made a great and lasting impression on him; and in declining years, when writing to a friend, he said, 'I shall like to hear a word about my dear old France, dear to me from childish associations.'

In 1821 Edward was sent to the Grammar School at Bury St. Edmunds, whither his brothers John and Peter had preceded him. This school, over which Dr. Malkin most successfully presided more than twenty years,

Edward Fitz-Gerald

had won a great reputation for scholarship. I know nothing of Fitz-Gerald's first impressions, but it does not appear that either he or his brothers attained particular distinction in the school. Being a dreamy boy, he was no adept at games; athletic exercises had no attractions for him, pastimes did not fall in with the peculiar bent of his mind. He was thus cut off from some of the roads to popularity in a public school, whilst his sensitive nature and shy disposition deprived him of companionship that he might otherwise have enjoyed. For all this, he had the attractive qualities upon which friendships are based. The commonplace lacks that winning force which first elicits, and then retains confidence. Birds of a feather will flock together, but everything depends upon the 'feather'; for congenial tastes, when uninspired by genius, rarely mingle for any length of time. Fitz-Gerald found sympathetic natures amongst those by whom he was surrounded. Here

The Life of

was begun the nucleus of those affectionate alliances which became so conspicuous a feature in his career. James Spedding, the well-known apologist of Lord Bacon; William Bodham Donne, who years after succeeded Kemble as Examiner of Plays; William Airy, brother of the late Astronomer-Royal; and John Mitchell Kemble, who afterwards stood in the front rank of those who drew the attention of the world to the treasures of Anglo-Saxon literature,—these were friends whose warmth of attachment was unaffected by lapse of time, or by the cooling tendency of engrossing occupations.

One of his brothers, Peter, left some remembrances among his schoolfellows, by which it is evident that he exhibited, both in and out of school, eccentricities which in after-life more or less characterised the entire family. After the death of Peter in 1875, Edward described him as an amiable gentleman with something helpless about

Edward Fitz-Gerald

him, what the Irish call an 'innocent man.' That this trait in his boyhood was constant may be inferred from the following record: —Peter Fitz-Gerald was one day brought before the master for misconduct out of school. When residing at Bredfield House, boy though he was, he had been sometimes allowed to drive his mother's four-in-hand, and when at school he greatly missed this diversion. To indulge this craving, he took to walking some five or six miles on the high-road till he met the London coach, when, by a previous arrangement with the coachman, he was allowed to have a box seat, to take the reins, and to drive into Bury St. Edmunds. His amateur driving was sometimes reckless, and, as may be inferred, was not agreeable to the passengers. As their appeals to the coachman failed, remonstrances were made to the head-master, and it was stated that the passengers feared an accident. Dr. Malkin forbade Master Peter again to drive the coach, and

The Life of

it was thought that his diversion in this particular line was at an end. Not so, however. The young gentleman was not so easily disconcerted. Subsequent representations were made to the Doctor, that Master Peter had been seen, in habiliments of woe, driving a hearse with four horses, carrying handsome plumes. To this remonstrance, the Doctor drily replied, 'I don't see that I need interfere unless the passenger complained.'

Having gained something more than an elementary knowledge of Greek and Latin, the time was considered to have arrived for Fitz-Gerald to commence a University career, and in 1826 he was entered at Trinity College, Cambridge. Peacock, an excellent teacher, was public tutor on his side, the other College tutors being Whewell and Higman; and Wordsworth, brother of the poet, was Master of Trinity. As to his College life, little is known beyond the fact that he was indolent, and spent his time in

Edward Fitz-Gerald

amusing himself rather than in pursuing regular studies. He exhibited no ambition for University distinction, and cared nothing for College honours. During his undergraduate career he increased his list of friends, and throughout life was better known for the friendships which he made whilst at Cambridge than for his efforts to obtain academic distinction. There it was that he first met Thackeray; W. H. Thompson, who succeeded Dr. Whewell in the Mastership of Trinity College; and John Allen, afterwards Archdeacon of Salop. The three Tennysons were added to his group of friends, but not till after he left Cambridge. He saw Alfred Tennyson as an undergraduate, but had no knowledge of him. In a letter to Mrs. Richmond Ritchie in 1882, in answer to inquiries about the Poet Laureate, he says: 'I did not know him till my College days were over.'

His College life was passed almost as a

holiday. His reading was discursive and sportive. Indulgences and impulses consumed the time that should have been given to systematic study; and as a natural consequence, when examination was due he was not at all prepared for it. Ten years afterwards he lamented this want of application during his residence at Cambridge. The editor of his *Letters* says that he passed through his University course in a leisurely manner, amusing himself with music, drawing, and poetry, and modestly went out in the poll in January 1830, after a period of suspense, during which he was apprehensive of not passing at all, though it does not appear that this would have caused him much distress. Thackeray, who was one of his greatest chums at Cambridge, was also extremely indolent, and left College without taking a degree; but Allen, quite a bosom friend, was a student in the true sense of the term, and though heavily handicapped by the death of his father

Edward Fitz-Gerald

two or three days before the examination, came out very creditably among the Senior Optimes.

Cambridge life at the time Fitz-Gerald entered the University was very different from what it is now. There was no pleasant intercourse between professor and students; to all appearance a great gulf divided them. Tennyson, speaking of his undergraduate days, says that the studies of the University were uninteresting, and 'none but dry-headed, calculating, angular little gentlemen can take delight in them. The dinners in Hall at Trinity at the undergraduates' tables were badly managed. The joints were put on the table to be hacked at by young men who knew nothing of carving,'[1] and the waiting was altogether insufficient for comfort. Sometimes three or four of the undergraduates would agree to have a quiet dinner in the rooms of one of them, each contributing, picnic-fashion, a share of the bill of

[1] Pollock's *Personal Remembrances.*

fare. This was much more enjoyable, but in getting dinners from the kitchen they were at times seen by one or more of the Dons, and this led to unpleasantness the following day. Athletics, in the sense in which the term is now used, were unknown, and boating on the river was almost the only exercise adopted. Many of the rowing men regularly appeared in tattered gowns and crushed caps, with green cut-away coats and red neckerchiefs, and some of the students took long walks in the country as 'constitutionals.'

The undergraduates met in one or another's rooms almost every evening, at which gatherings much coffee was drunk, much tobacco smoked, and discussion on a variety of subjects pursued. In the *Life of Archdeacon Allen* mention is made of these meetings, and of the fun indulged in among the friends of his circle, which included Fitz-Gerald, Spedding, and Thackeray. Fitz-Gerald was all frolic, scattering

Edward Fitz-Gerald

his smart sayings about with the greatest freedom. Thackeray, with his sarcasm and his wit, was equally striking, though more sedate in his delivery, whilst Spedding was ofttimes anxious to discuss critical points in the writings of Bacon or Shakespeare.

The writer in the *Edinburgh Review* (1894) when referring to Fitz-Gerald's friends and College chums says: 'Cambridge has not produced in this century their equals. None of them, indeed, played that conspicuous part in public life which distinguished their more ambitious Oxford contemporaries, but they were all men of the highest literary culture, of refined taste and originality.' And Lord Houghton, speaking in 1866 at the opening of the 'New Cambridge Union' of the men who were friends and associates of Fitz-Gerald and Tennyson, said: 'I am inclined to believe that the members of that generation were, for the wealth of their promise, a rare body of men, such as this University has seldom contained.'

The Life of

In addition to those I have named, the men at Cambridge with whom he was on intimate terms included Trench (afterwards Archbishop of Dublin), Alford (afterwards Dean of Canterbury), Merivale (afterwards Dean of Ely), Blakesley (afterwards Dean of Lincoln), Charles Buller, Spring, Rice, and others, the mention of whose names is sufficient to show that Fitz-Gerald's friends at the University were among those who distinguished themselves in the world of literature. If a man is known by the company he keeps, Fitz-Gerald's place among contemporaries speaks for itself.

Leaving Cambridge and the friends of his undergraduate days, he entered into that conventional circle which certainly did not feel the want of a man who disregarded its manners, defied many of its customs, and was full of Utopian ideas. For a time he stayed with his brother-in-law, Mr. Kerrich of Geldeston Hall, near Beccles; and from his frequent visits there at later periods,

Edward Fitz-Gerald

this was evidently a favourite retreat in which to enjoy his free-and-easy life. After a few months he went to Paris on a visit to his aunt Miss Purcell, where Thackeray joined him. We have seen that Thackeray was one of Fitz-Gerald's College chums—one whose affections clung to him at Cambridge, and for years after. He was two years younger than Fitz-Gerald, but quitted College in the same year. Behind him he left a reputation for burlesque verses and impromptu pen-and-ink sketches of the Hogarth kind rather than for hard study. The pair had lounged about London for a time, and Fitz-Gerald had not been long in Paris before Thackeray made his appearance, having, he said, resolved to become an artist. To qualify himself for his intended profession he commenced copying pictures in the Louvre, Fitz-Gerald being his companion; but he was constitutionally idle, and his friend was too indolent to urge him to 'improve the shining hour.' The result was that though his sketches, when he begun to work for himself, were clever, he never became proficient in drawing the human figure.

Fitz-Gerald wrote to Allen telling him of the pictures and statues, and expressing a wish that he would come and join them. He adds: 'You must know I am going to become a great bear, and have got all sorts of Utopian ideas in my head about society.'

Coming back to England, Fitz-Gerald for several weeks made Southampton his head-quarters, in order that he might pay a few flying visits to some College friends, and went to Salisbury, ostensibly to see the Cathedral, but really to make a pilgrimage to Bemerton—George Herbert's home.

Before the end of the year he went to Northamptonshire, staying for a time in the village of Naseby, where his father had an estate which included the very field in which a crushing defeat broke the hopes of Charles I. This retreat interested him

Edward Fitz-Gerald

much. He settled down in 'a nice farmhouse,' and wrote to Allen, 'Can't you come? I am quite the king here, I promise you.' One day he dines with the estate carpenter, 'whose daughter plays on the pianoforte. . . . My blue surtout daily does wonders. At church its effect is truly delightful.'

Allen left Cambridge in 1832, and soon after went to stay with relatives in a country house called Freestone, a few miles from Tenby. A short time only elapsed before Fitz-Gerald received an invitation to visit him, and to this he very readily responded, and journeyed to Tenby, in which little seaport town he took lodgings. The two friends felt as if they could not bear separation; they were like schoolboys in their delight in each other's company. They walked daily to meet one another on the road, and wandered among the rocks and along the coast, or enjoyed the most friendly hospitality at Freestone, extended

The Life of

over several weeks in the summer and autumn of that year. Fitz-Gerald always looked back with delight to this outing, which formed a series of red-letter days in his calendar.

Returning to London, he moved about amongst divers booksellers' shops, and bought Bacon's *Essays*, Brown's *Religio Medici*, etc., to add to his collection, which had stood still of late. He also hunted for an ancient drinking-cup, which he might use 'when I am in my house in quality of housekeeper.' Thackeray dropped in, and helped to drive away his blue devils, but the satirist was very soon off again to Devonshire. One of Fitz-Gerald's sisters was with him in London, and they trudged about to see its sights. In the following year he took lodgings in Bloomsbury, and was a frequent visitor to the British Museum. He spent the May term of 1834 at Cambridge, 'rejoicing in the sunshine of James Spedding's presence,' and thence he jour-

Edward Fitz-Gerald

neyed to the residence of his father, Wherstead Lodge, near Ipswich.

This Wherstead Lodge, a charming residence on the west side of the Orwell, and about two miles from Ipswich, had been occupied by Mr. Fitz-Gerald for several years. The mansion, which commands delightful views of the river and the surrounding country, was built by Sir Robert Harland towards the end of the last century. Externally it lacks architectural pretensions, but the hall and staircase are both imposing, the effect being heightened by a splendid collection of pictures, which include a large number of valuable portraits from the easels of Zucchero, Hogarth, Cosway, Sir Godfrey Kneller, Sir Peter Lely, and Sir Joshua Reynolds. In the hall was the last of the six very elaborately adorned chairs of ebony profusely inlaid with ivory, which the Nabob of Arcot in 1772 gave to Lady Harland; the other five were sold to George IV. for his pavilion at Brighton. Prior to Mr. Fitz-

Gerald's occupation of Wherstead Lodge, it was let to Lord Granville for £1000 a year with the shooting; and during his lordship's tenancy some of the most eminent nobles, statesmen, courtiers, and financial princes of his era were among the visitors. The church stands in the park, and the churchyard, which is nearly one hundred feet above the level of the river, commands without exception a view of the most beautiful piece of scenery in the eastern counties. At high water the Orwell from this point has more the appearance of a long lake than a river; and the woods of the neighbouring parks, falling one into the other in almost unbroken line, catch the eye and appeal to the imagination.

Mr. Fitz-Gerald's occupancy of such a house for many years was a guarantee of his wealth; and it will readily be supposed that his son Edward would be delighted by its contents and the charms of the scenery. Writing from Wherstead in the

Edward Fitz-Gerald

summer of 1834, he boasts of brave health, of being an early riser, and useful as a pruner of roses. To him the spot was a paradise; and he writes to Allen, 'All our family, except my mother, are collected here, all my brothers and sisters, with their wives, husbands, and children sitting at different occupations, or wandering about the grounds and gardens, discoursing each their separate concerns, but all united into one whole.' This gathering of the family seems to have been a prelude to Mr. Fitz-Gerald's leaving Wherstead Lodge, as Edward writes to Thackeray, who was then in Paris, 'My father is determined to inhabit Boulge Hall, an empty house of his, about fourteen miles off, and we are very sorry to leave this really beautiful place.' Edward mentions that he is likely to remain in Suffolk all the winter, because two of his sisters are to inhabit alone the old mansion to which they were removing, and he intended to keep them company.

The Life of

His days at Wherstead were full of pleasant memories, to which he frequently referred, and he and his sisters left that favoured spot with keen regret.

In the early part of 1835 he went to Cumberland and spent a few weeks at Mirehouse on Bassenthwaite Lake, the home of his dear friend James Spedding, the pleasure of the visit being greatly enhanced by finding Alfred Tennyson also a guest. At what date, or under what circumstances, Fitz-Gerald became acquainted with Tennyson, I know not. Waugh in his *Life of Tennyson* says that the poet and Fitz-Gerald became friends in 1835. Upon what authority this statement is made does not appear. The present Lord Tennyson, writing to me, says, 'I know not when Fitz-Gerald and my father first met.' It is therefore probable that Spedding as a mutual friend was the medium of introduction. In a letter written in May 1835 to John Allen, Fitz-Gerald simply says, ' Alfred

Edward Fitz-Gerald

Tennyson stayed with me in Cumberland.' This shows that they were known to each other before that period. Writing to W. B. Donne, he says, 'Tennyson has been in town for some time; he has been making fresh poems, which are finer they say than anything he has done.' May we not infer that he had already made acquaintance with the poet? At any rate, the visit to the Lakes firmly cemented a friendship which was lifelong, and Alfred Tennyson henceforth became one of those friends to whom Fitz-Gerald was knit as to a brother.

Spedding's father, who was a fine example of a north-country gentleman, farmed a great portion of his own estate, and the property was said to have much increased in value from his judicious management. Early hours were kept, and the elder Spedding mounted his cob after breakfast, and was about his farm till dinner at two. There was a serious tea after dinner, which was the great time for talk and discussion.

The Life of

After tea the father 'sat reading by a shaded lamp, saying very little, but always courteous, and quite content with any company his son might bring to the house, so long as they let him go his way, which indeed he would have gone whether they let him or no. But he had seen enough of poets not to like them or their trade—Shelley for a time living among the Lakes, Coleridge at Southey's (whom perhaps he had a respect for), and Wordsworth, whom I don't think he valued. He was rather jealous of "Jem," who might have done available service in the world, he thought, instead of giving himself up to such dreamers, and sitting up with Tennyson and Fitz-Gerald at night, when all the house was mute, conning over the "Morte d'Arthur," "Dora," "Lord of Burleigh," and other poems, which helped to make up the two volumes of 1842. So I always associate that Arthur Idyll with Bassenthwaite Lake under Skiddaw. Mrs. Spedding was a sensible motherly lady with

Edward Fitz-Gerald

whom I used to play chess of an evening. And there was an old friend of hers, Mrs. Bristow, who always reminded me of Miss La Creevy, if you know of such a person in *Nickleby.*'[1]

At this house Fitz-Gerald was very happy. He and his companions rambled about without definite aim. Sometimes they strolled into the woods in the neighbourhood of Mirehouse; sometimes they had a boat on the lake. There was always something to attract them; the soft luxuriance of the scenery was an ever-abiding source of delight. Fertile imaginations in such surroundings are never at a loss for objects to admire; their enchantments multiply; charm follows charm; nature is exhaustless in its varying moods; the poetic fancy revels in the riches spread out before it, and to such the barren field would be clothed with beauty of its own. At the end of May the party went to lodge for a week

[1] Fitz-Gerald's *Letters to Fanny Kemble.*

at Windermere, where Spedding had to leave them; whilst there Wordsworth's new volume of *Yarrow Revisited* came to hand. Wordsworth was then at home; but Fitz-Gerald says: 'Tennyson would not go to visit him, and, of course, I did not, nor even saw him.'[1] Spedding, speaking of this visit to the Lake country in a letter to Thompson, said: 'I could not get Alfred to Rydal Mount. He would, and would not (sulky one), although Wordsworth was hospitably inclined towards him.' Lord Tennyson in his *Biography of the Poet Laureate*, alluding to this statement of Spedding's, says that his father did not like to intrude himself on the great man at Rydal. Spedding, in the letter just quoted, said: 'I think Tennyson took in more pleasure and inspiration in this visit to the Lakes than any one would have supposed who did not know his own almost personal dislike of the present, whatever that may be.'

[1] Fitz-Gerald's *Letters to Fanny Kemble*.

Edward Fitz-Gerald

By no one were the beauties of the Lake district more exquisitely enjoyed than by Fitz-Gerald; and this visit served the double purpose of drawing out his heart to external charms, which, although unemotional in themselves, excited boundless joys in himself, and of deepening and cementing his acquaintance with Tennyson. The love of nature and the love of a friend could not have been more happily combined. When relating their rambles in a letter of this date to his friend Allen, he says: 'I will say no more of Tennyson than that the more I have seen of him, the more cause I have to think him great. His little humours and grumpiness were so droll, that I was always laughing. I felt what Charles Lamb described a sense of depression at times, from the overshadowing of a so much more lofty intellect than my own. Perhaps I have received some benefit in the now more distinct consciousness of my own dwarfishness.' This pouring out his own secrets shows that his

The Life of

friendship with Allen was unique. Between the two there was an ideal bond of sympathy and affection. Such a tie must have bound Cicero to his friend Scipio, and knit the soul of David and Jonathan. Friendship of this sort has been defined as one soul in two bodies.

For two or three years Fitz-Gerald seems to have flitted from place to place. In the spring of 1839 he was at Geldestone, where he lived, as he said, in a very seedy manner. Geldestone Hall was Liberty Hall to him; he could come and go as he liked; and at night after supper could retire to the kitchen to read Harrington's *Oceana* and smoke until midnight.

Later in the year he was in the land of John Bunyan, spending time with his friend Browne at Bedford. The acquaintance with this gentleman began in a boarding-house at Tenby some years previous, and was kept up with mutual interest, though those that knew the two men could scarcely

Edward Fitz-Gerald

suppose that there was much in common between them: Fitz-Gerald, a man thoroughly fond of books, a master of several languages, a recluse by habit, and totally averse to taking any part even in his duties as a citizen: Browne, on the other hand, a man in the full enjoyment of life, quick to love and quick to fight, a business man, who became an officer in the militia, and joined heartily in the political battles of the town of Bedford, who was elected member of the Corporate Body, and was moreover so keen a sportsman that his friend declared he was more intent on the first of September than on anything else in the world. Fitz-Gerald paid him an annual visit, invited him to stay at Lowestoft, and took him as companion on one of his visits to his uncle in Ireland. When at Bedford the friends went fishing, and after their day's enjoyment had tea at a roadside inn, as Fitz-Gerald preferred taking apartments to staying at his friend's house. During these outings he took a drawing-

The Life of

book and a colour-box with him to make sketches of the quiet scenery on the banks of the Ouse.

Mr. Browne's marriage to a wealthy lady greatly concerned Fitz-Gerald, who expressed a hope that his friend would not be defiled by the filthy pitch.

That his shyness passed away in those early days whenever he was with staunch friends is evident from anecdotes which now and then find their way into print. The year of the Queen's Coronation (1838) was very loyally celebrated by a small coterie of Cambridge men, consisting of Fitz-Gerald, Spedding, Douglas Heath, and W. F. Pollock (son of Sir Frederick Pollock), at Kitlands, close to Leith Hill in Surrey, where Sergeant Heath had built a charming house and laid out some lovely grounds. Douglas Heath was a private tutor at Trinity College, Pollock was one of his pupils, probably Spedding and Fitz-Gerald bore the same relation, and hence they were

Edward Fitz-Gerald

invited to form the party which went down to Kitlands the evening before. In the early part of the afternoon on the 28th of June, a beautiful warm day, the four were assembled on the edges of a long, open bath which lay in the garden, surrounded by thick bushes, a most tempting spot for the purpose. As the hour for placing the crown on the Queen's head in Westminster Abbey approached, they made ready for a plunge; and when the sound of the distant cannon reached them, all took headers into the water and swam about singing 'God save the Queen.'[1] Those who knew Fitz-Gerald late in life would never have supposed that the eccentric recluse of Woodbridge, who sometimes brusquely declined to see a friend, would have joined in such rollicking capers even at the most skittish time of life, or in connection with a rare incident of national interest.

At the period at which I have now

[1] Sir F. Pollock's *Personal Remembrances.*

The Life of

arrived Fitz-Gerald made a new acquaintance, which, like those formed at school and at the University, was lifelong. Mr. Samuel Laurence, an artist residing in London, was introduced to Fitz-Gerald by his friend Spedding as an artist of ability, and of worth as a man. After a friendship of more than forty years, Fitz-Gerald could say that he had proved the truth of these testimonies, and the *last* letter which he is known to have penned was sent to Samuel Laurence. I give here a copy of his *first* letter to that gentleman :—

'*Sept.* 10*th*, '38. BOULGE HALL.

'DEAR SIR,—William Browne, whose face you will remember, wishes to see John Allen's portrait. He could, I know, have accomplished this without any introductory letter from me, but I am glad of the opportunity of saying a few words to you. I assure you, I have thought with very much pleasure, and a very many times, of the new

Edward Fitz-Gerald

acquaintance I have made with you; and it is with some such hope that it may not die away, that I am tempted to send you these few lines. When I shall be in London again I cannot say, but I conclude before much time has elapsed. I have been spending all this summer with this identical W. Browne, and sorry I am to part with him. We have been fishing, and travelling about in a gig as happy as needs be. I should like to hear that you had been getting the fresh air in some such holiday-making, for I cannot but think both eye and hand and the directing mind require some such relaxation. All these lose their best impulses by being used too slavishly. But all this you knew before.

'I have still a vision of Rome floating before me, and something tells me that if I don't go this winter I never shall. And yet what between my own indecision, and a few cross casualties, I am sure I shall not accomplish it. I have seen two cartoons said to be by Raffaelle: one of the well-known vision of Ezekiel; the other of a Holy Family, both at a place of the Duke of Buccleuch in Northamptonshire. I did not know whether to think them original or not. I suppose a visit to Rome, or an exact technical knowledge of pictures, is very essential. I am sure I can understand the finest part of pictures without doing either.

'I sincerely wish you health and all good things, and am yours very truly,

'E. FITZ-GERALD.'

Fitz-Gerald was fond of art, had a fair knowledge of pictures by the Old Masters, as well as of the English School, and oft-times tried his hand at sketching. In the *Life of Lord Tennyson* by his son there is an engraving from a chalk drawing by Fitz-Gerald, showing a back view of Alfred Tennyson's head and shoulders, taken when he and Fitz-Gerald were on a visit to James

Edward Fitz-Gerald

Spedding at his Cumberland home. When at Naseby, and also when with his friend Browne at Bedford, Fitz-Gerald spent part of his time in making water-colour sketches, which he said, in writing to Laurence, 'will make you throw down your brush in despair.' An artist who was clever and thoroughly honest was just such a friend as Fitz-Gerald really wanted; and as I have stated, one of his firmest friendships followed his acquaintance with Laurence. Fitz-Gerald was a frequent correspondent, and complained at times that some of his friends did not reply so often as he wished. Laurence, on the contrary, was very prompt, and at short intervals he received inquiries and commissions. At one time he is requested to go to Colnaghi's and get a new lithographic print of a head of Dante, after a fresco by Giotti, lately discovered in Florence — the most wonderful head ever seen, Dante about twenty-seven years old. Later he is told 'to keep his eye on the little Titian' which

The Life of

Fitz-Gerald wants to purchase of a London dealer, and said, 'I shall make the venture of borrowing £30 to invest in it: I may never be able to get a bit of Titian in my life again.'

Generous to a fault, he was safe to pay for all trouble he occasioned, so that he took care to recommend his friend Laurence as a portrait-painter, and several commissions were the result. In October 1843 he wrote to Laurence: 'I purpose to live the winter in Ipswich. You must come and see me at Christmas. I shall be able to get you a commission or two, for I am considered rather an authority in these parts.' This was one of the ideas which he did not carry out, as I never heard of his living in Ipswich, but he frequently gave commissions to the artist himself. He was always anxious to have portraits of his dearest friends hanging on the walls of his home. That of Lord Tennyson, which forms the frontispiece to the *Life* by his son, was

Edward Fitz-Gerald

painted by Laurence for Fitz-Gerald, as well as portraits of Archdeacon Allen, and of Thackeray. He wished for a portrait of his great favourite—the poet Crabbe; and Pickersgill's portrait, in the possession of Crabbe's grandson, was borrowed for the purpose. It was suggested to him that a copy of Phillip's portrait would look well; but his reply was, 'No—Phillip's portrait just represents what I least wanted—Crabbe's *company look*, whereas Pickersgill's represents the Thinker!'

One of the peculiarities of his life was his adoption of a vegetarian diet, though the pleasures of the table were at no time any particular attraction to him. This peculiarity did not consist so much in his abstinence from a flesh diet as in the manner in which he carried out his scheme. He commenced this experiment about 1833, when he was twenty-four years of age, a wrong time, as he said, to begin a change of that kind. Doubts and difficulties were pressed upon his notice by intimate friends, but he kept on, determined to give the system a fair trial. He was not in bondage to a beefsteak or a mutton-chop, and, as we know, was rather anxious than not to depart in some things from the ways of so-called good society. Loss of physical power for a time followed the experiment, but he did not get frightened by the suggestion that his strength was ebbing away. He persevered, upheld as he was by an almost fanatical notion that abstinence from a flesh diet would produce greater simplicity of life, and give the soul a strong command over the body. At the end of four months he acknowledged that he had found no benefit beyond more lightness of spirits. He lived chiefly on bread eaten with fruit, pears and apples being the chief articles of consumption, as he had no faith in green vegetables. To this kind of diet, with occasional exceptions, he adhered for the remainder of his life, and certainly maintained a fair state of health.

Edward Fitz-Gerald

I have said that he occasionally broke through his vegetarian rule, and these exceptions exhibit in a marked way the peculiarity of the man. During the early days of his experiment he attended a dinner-party and partook of meat. He was not seduced by roast partridge and bread sauce, but he did not like to look singular, and found it much easier to conform than to have the courage of his convictions. Late in life, ducks could be seen swimming in the small pond in the garden of his house at Woodbridge; and when a friend dropped in to dine with him in summer-time, duck and green peas were brought to table for the friend, whilst Fitz-Gerald himself sat eating fruit, and discussed with him the literature of the day. If he stopped to supper at a friend's house (which, by the bye, was seldom), he did not object to partaking of a little fish, or fowl, or game. As far as *principle* was concerned, there was no adherence to vegetarianism. As presents to a friend he did not hesitate to send a turkey or a brace of pheasants. In one letter he says, 'I have just written your name and address on a parchment label, which is to show a goose the way to your kitchen'; in another, 'I have bid them send you a small turkey, and some country sausages for garnish'; and in an early letter to Laurence he writes, 'I wish you were here to eat my turkey with me.' It is thus clear that he was a very accommodating vegetarian; and when such friends as Lord Tennyson or W. F. Pollock were his visitors, he took care that they should be well provided for as to bed and board, regardless of expense, at the best hotel in Woodbridge. Still, in the main, for his own sustenance he was a vegetarian; and three years before his death, when writing to Fanny Kemble, he said as to meals, 'tea, pure and simple, with bread-and-butter, is the only meal I do care to join in.'

Edward Fitz-Gerald

FITZ-GERALD BECOMES A HOUSEKEEPER

FITZ-GERALD'S life, from the time he left College till he was nearly thirty years of age, was chiefly spent in rambling about the country with different friends, or in staying for short periods with his relatives; but then, it seems, he grew tired of roaming, and longed for a home of his own. His father and family were living at Boulge Hall; and in 1837 he gave indications to a friend that he was preparing to settle close by the Hall, and spoke of a small cottage which was just outside the park gates as a suitable residence. A few months later his ideas had developed, and he was living at the cottage, where he could say, 'I have my books, a barrel of beer, which I tap myself, and an old woman to do for me.' This village of Boulge, one of the smallest in Suffolk, is about two miles from Woodbridge, and adjoins Bredfield, where Fitz-Gerald was born. It had only eight inhabited houses, and the residents, including those at the Hall, numbered fewer than fifty. Fitz-Gerald acknowledged that the village was one of the dullest places in England; the principal objects of its landscape were pollard trees, overlooking a flat country with regular hedges.

If Fitz-Gerald trudged from the village to Woodbridge, he encountered no bustle to jar his nerves. He was strongly attached to this quiet little town, and had walked to it from Bredfield and Boulge so often, that every field and tree along the road was as familiar to him as were his books. When he first became acquainted with the physical aspects of Woodbridge, neither the lighting nor the paving of the town commanded the admiration of strangers. Gas was not in

Edward Fitz-Gerald

use; puny oil lamps were few and far between; dingy lights in shop windows tended to make darkness more visible. The streets were lined with irregular but picturesque structures, mixed with the trim built and uniform houses of modern times. Except on market days, the town might have been described as a very sleepy place, but on those days it woke up, and for a few hours was full of activity. It seemed as if all the squires and parsons, with their wives and daughters, for miles around gravitated thither. Their vehicles were known to every tradesman; the parsons themselves appeared to know everybody. For Fitz-Gerald, who loved to be 'far from the madding crowd,' this town, within touch of his new abode, was a delight in many ways; he was never tired of expressing his admiration of the river, on which he frequently enjoyed himself when bound for sea.

His cottage was quaint-looking, of one story, with an unusually low-pitched thatched roof. It was never celebrated for accommodation, and remains much as it was half a century ago. In the centre is a door and passage, with a room on each side, used by him as parlour and bedroom. He said that 'the walls were as thin as a sixpence'; its windows were difficult to shut. There were no eave-troughs to carry off the water, and as it stood on clay soil, the house was damp. It will not excite surprise to find that in such a tenement he had three attacks of influenza. Here he resided twelve or fourteen years, having little to divert him in the outside world beside geese in the meadow, the butcher's boy rattling along with his cart as if it were a question of life and death, and the washerwoman trundling her weary load. Still he had a strong liking for this doleful place, and did something towards giving a cosy and domestic look to its interior. The walls of the two rooms were papered with a still green to suit his pictures, his books were on

Edward Fitz-Gerald

ranges of shelves, a charming engraving of Stothard's 'Canterbury Pilgrims' hung over the fireplace, a bust of Shakespeare was in a recess. He delighted to see these things; and after his homely dinner it was his custom to read and smoke by the fire with a dog on the hearthrug, his love of animals and his own contentment being typified by his unconscious caress of a sleeping cat, curled up on a chair beside him. In the kitchen was an old woman who superintended his household; and, after a visit to London, the return to this primitive country house was one of his greatest pleasures.

It must not be thought from this description that Fitz-Gerald was an adept at methodical arrangement in a house. Every one who knew this genius would scout such an idea. Even a cursory peep into the room was enough to show that disorder was a conspicuous feature. Some of the bookshelves extended from the floor nearly to the ceiling. Quartos and octavos were

The Life of

ranged side by side; but as the shelves would not contain all his precious books, the floor was made use of, and large volumes were heaped together in confusion. The air of the room, though strongly impregnated with the scent of tobacco, was musty, as he objected to cleaning, and would not have the books dusted; his old woman, he said, would put them back in what she called orderly fashion, and it would be weeks before he knew where to find what he wanted. It may easily be imagined that in such a room accommodation for visitors was not always to be found; they had ofttimes to be content with the ledge of a bookshelf; and so taken up were the chairs by pictures and books, that the master of the house himself had apparently to take his meals standing. This congested condition might have been partly avoided by driving a few nails in the walls and rearranging the furniture, but the occupant was not handy at any mechanical turn. If

Edward Fitz-Gerald

he tried to knock in a nail, his fingers were likely to receive the blow. He gave up shaving himself, as he drew blood frequently, and engaged a Woodbridge man, who was both letter-carrier and barber, to perform the operation for him three times a week.

That this sketch is not at all overdrawn will be seen by the following letter from a lady who knew him well. She says :—

'My father drove my mother and myself as a child in his gig one summer's evening to Boulge. Fitz-Gerald then occupied the cottage at the Hall gates. It was a bungalow thatched. The chaos of the room is vividly in my mind. Large pictures standing against the walls. Portrait on an easel, books, boots, sticks, music scattered about on tables, chairs, and floor. An open piano with music, lumber everywhere, so that there was a difficulty in emptying a chair for my mother to sit on. He himself had let us in, in dressing-gown and slippers.'

In connection with his life at the cottage,

The Life of

it may be mentioned that although Fitz-Gerald was not enamoured with the Service of the Church of England, or that of any other sect, he in early life ofttimes attended the parish church on Sundays in conformity with custom. When he left his cottage to stay a week or two with his father and mother at the Hall, he invariably went to church with the family party. Service began at half-past ten, and when his visit was in cold weather he wrapped himself up in a greatcoat to keep out the damp, as he said toadstools grew round the Communion Table.

It was about this time that there crossed the path of Fitz-Gerald a man who, for the next twenty years, shed a happy influence on his life. This was the Rev. George Crabbe, eldest son and biographer of the very poet whom Fitz-Gerald almost idolised. This gentleman was presented to the vicarage of the adjoining parish of Bredfield; and between the two men, who had

Edward Fitz-Gerald

much in common (both being haters of shams and of some of the conventionalities of society), a friendship sprang up which was a great blessing to both of them, and only terminated by the death of Mr. Crabbe. Fitz-Gerald always spoke of this friend as a capital fellow, who, with 'manhood's energy of mind and great bodily strength, united the boy's heart, and was as much a boy at seventy as boys need be at seventeen. He was careless of riches, intolerant of injustice and oppression, and incapable of all that is base, little, or mean.' Mr. Crabbe was very like his father in features, but detested poetry. This feeling was so strong that he had actually never read all his father's poems till a few years before his death, when Fitz-Gerald induced him to do so. He was old-fashioned in his notions; and when Dr. Whewell's book on the *Plurality of Worlds* was published, he read it with avidity, but 'most indignantly rejected the doctrine as unworthy of God.'

The Life of

Boulge Cottage was about a mile from Bredfield Vicarage, and Fitz-Gerald frequently lighted a lantern about seven in the evening of a winter's night and trudged through the mud to spend a few hours with the parson. Sometimes he stopped the night, when they discussed Paley's *Theology*, or exchanged views upon the then burning Gorham question. Music was one of the elements of their union; and with the help of the vicar's son and daughter, Fitz-Gerald was ambitious enough to try Handel's *Coronation Anthems*, though he admitted they had not a voice among them. Occasionally, before starting homeward with his lantern, he would play one of Handel's Overtures, and then join in glees. On New Year's Eve he would walk over to Bredfield to sit with his friend and smoke out the Old Year. Sometimes the parson might be seen with a cigar in his mouth, wending his way to the cottage for a gossip. The home of each was perfectly open to the other.

Edward Fitz-Gerald

In the autumn of 1857 this friendship was dissolved. Crabbe died from an epileptic fit; and Fitz-Gerald, who was away in Bedfordshire, hurried back to attend the funeral. It was sad enough under such circumstances to revisit the house in which he had spent so many enjoyable hours. The dear friend who had so often welcomed him now lay cold in his coffin. Death having been sudden, the room smelt strongly of tobacco, and the last cheroot he had tried lay three-quarters burnt in its little china ashpan. This and a silver nutmeg grater, which had often been used during their evening gossips, Fitz-Gerald took and cherished as relics of his departed friend.

During the life of Mr. Crabbe, Fitz-Gerald occasionally met two or three acquaintances at the vicar's table; and after this he seemed desirous of imitating Charles Lamb by having a few friends to supper and sometimes to dinner at the 'Bungalow.' There was this difference, however, whilst

The Life of

Lamb had an open house one evening in the week, Fitz-Gerald's party were always invited, and usually consisted of Archdeacon Groome, Rev. George Crabbe, Bernard Barton, Francis Capper Brooke, Thomas Churchyard, or one or two others in place of them. These entertainments at the cottage were spoken of as hospitable but not comfortable, as Fitz-Gerald would not ring for his servant to come and help. But he was very pleased with the result of his gatherings. He told one friend that the guests who assembled round his table were looked upon as the chief wits of Woodbridge, and one man had said to him that 'he envied our conversations.' He clearly anticipated that these small gatherings would become opportunities for mental diversion, and so probably they did with such men as he got together. The very form of the invitation reminded you of the man: 'Won't ye come to me on Tuesday? so-and-so will be here. Come if you can.' One who had

Edward Fitz-Gerald

been his guest says : 'When there you found yourself face to face with tried friends or chosen companions of him, who knew what cultured conversation meant, and gathered round his board those who had a kindred taste. And if at the head of the table there was a studied defiance of some of the little conventionalities which are supposed to make the wheels of society run smooth, if in dress or appliances there was something a little strange, none left the table without a feeling that he had been the guest of one who, disregarding the tinsel, thoroughly knew and practised the real refinement of an English gentleman.' As he enjoyed these gatherings, it shows that he was not then the hermit which he ultimately became.

Fitz-Gerald made no pretence as a host. He enjoyed providing supper for his guests, but paid no regard to the niceties of housekeeping. His cottage home occupied but little of his attention; domestic comfort scarcely troubled him; he found the money, but his housekeeper spent it. In his own neighbourhood he was considered a recluse; to the unlearned labourer he was a mystery. Many misunderstood him, and therefore could not make allowances for his idiosyncrasies, hence he frequently went away from home in search of the sympathy he craved.

His simple and unpretending manners were little in sympathy with the conventional mode of living, hence he refrained from associating with county society. He was not the man to adopt the stiff and meaningless ceremony of paying and receiving calls, though to this rule, as to many others, he made exceptions. Fitz-Gerald had sometimes met Mr. Charles Austin of Brandeston Hall (the most successful leader of the Parliamentary Bar of his times) at the house of a mutual friend, Francis Capper Brooke of Ufford Place. When this gentleman married in 1856, Fitz-Gerald paid a visit of congratulation.

Edward Fitz-Gerald

Mr. and Mrs. Austin returned the call, but he was not at home, and thus the interchange of visits between these two began and ended.

Archdeacon Groome, who was rector of a village within a few miles of Woodbridge, was a lifelong friend of Fitz-Gerald's, and in many ways they were kindred spirits. He was a lover of music, a man of wide culture, who had read much but published little, a student of old English literature, and his acquaintance with early English MSS. was such as to render him an authority to whom one could go with confidence. The humour of the dialect and folklore of the county was appreciated by nobody more than by himself, and what added to the pleasure of his company was his felicity in capping verses; in this particular art he was, his son says, a master.

Mr. Churchyard of Woodbridge was known in the district as 'lawyer Churchyard,' by his intimates as Tom Churchyard.

The Life of

He was clever in many ways, was a conspicuous member of the legal profession, was a fluent speaker and persuasive pleader, an artist of no mean ability, and a well-read man. His professional work would have brought him affluence; but his art, which he loved more, weakened his devotion to the law. A man cannot worship successfully at two shrines. The easel put the parchment in the shade; he died poor, but was not neglected by Fitz-Gerald.

Bernard Barton, a highly esteemed resident in Woodbridge, was generally known as the Quaker Poet. He was a clerk in Messrs. Alexander and Co.'s bank from 1810 till his death in 1849. His first volume of poems was issued in 1812. This brought him into correspondence with Byron, Southey, Charles Lamb, Hogg the Ettrick Shepherd, and many others. He published many subsequent volumes, but the financial result was less satisfactory than that of a letter he sent to Sir Robert

Edward Fitz-Gerald

Peel on the income-tax, showing the way in which it unduly pressed upon a poor clerk's remuneration. Sir Robert was so pleased with this epistle, that he sent an invitation to the Quaker Poet to dine with him at Whitehall; and before he retired from office, he recommended him to the Queen as a fit subject for an annual pension of £100.

There was much about Bernard Barton calculated to excite the admiration of every lover of humanity. As a Quaker he was thoroughly consistent, but of far too genial a nature to stickle for the peculiarities of the Friends, and could forget 'thee' and 'thou,' when conversing with the world's people. A well-marked feature of his character, which was the very antithesis of Quakerism, was his love of humour. He admired it in his reading, and had a fund of his own upon which he was continually drawing. Even in Scott's novels he relished humour more than pathos. With a strong memory, his power of illustration was so good, that his conversation was a perpetual feast; lovers of literature were as much charmed by his abundant knowledge and felicity of expression as by his geniality in the social circle.

Some men in passing through life make many acquaintances, but few friends; they lack the confiding faculty, and confidence is the soul of friendship. On the other hand, men of keen sensibilities and thoughtful character generally limit their friendships to a small circle, and give to the members who compose it a friendship of the most exclusive, intimate, and unreserved kind. This was the case with Fitz-Gerald. His friendship was more like love. The persons to whom he was drawn by a kind of magnetic attraction were his companions in school and college days; and the confiding intimacies begun thus early caused each object of his regard to be pressed close to his heart, and embraced with a brother's love. His attachments were lifelong, and the friendships which intellectual habits and

Edward Fitz-Gerald

congeniality of disposition had helped to form defied all the vicissitudes of life, held good in all relations and conditions, and were for him not merely a soothing influence, but his greatest source of happiness. Taking his life as a whole, there were only a few of what are familiarly known as bright spots, but each friendship was like a fertile oasis in the desert of his existence. The gleams of joy and hope which occasionally shone across his gloomy path were due to the attachments he had formed with a few great minds who thoroughly understood the man.

Every now and then he journeyed to London, and it seemed as if Alfred Tennyson was the one friend he was most anxious to meet. Between them there was a great spirit of kinship, identity of opinion, and similarity of taste.

These visits to London sometimes extended to three or four weeks. There was no railway from his home in those days;

The Life of

and the journeys being to him rather formidable, he took care to make the most of them, and tried to see all his friends. He was always delighted to get among his Cambridge associates, who kept pretty well in touch with each other in the metropolis. Allen and Thackeray were both living in London, Spedding had rooms in Lincoln's Inn Fields, and Tennyson, who resided with his mother in Epping Forest, frequently spent the evening in London. Their house of call was the Cock Tavern, Temple Bar; and when with Spedding or Tennyson, the dinner consisted of a chop and pickle, cheese and stout, and a cigar or pipe. Spedding and Fitz-Gerald frequently paid a visit to the Royal Academy, or spent an evening at the theatre. But the greatest treats were the discussions in Spedding's room, in which the party sat up smoking till past midnight, when Tennyson, who was a good reciter, would be induced to give them some of 'his magic music,' and then to bed. This

Edward Fitz-Gerald

was about the happiest period of Fitz-Gerald's life.

At one of these meetings Fitz-Gerald's considerate thoughtfulness was a public advantage. Tennyson sometimes brought MS. or proofs to submit to his friends. Fitz-Gerald says 'the poems published in two vols. in 1842 were nearly all written out in a foolscap folio parchment bound book such as accounts are kept in (only not ruled). I used to call it the butcher's book.' The poems were written in Tennyson's very fine hand towards one side of the large paper, the unoccupied edges and corners being often torn off for pipelights, care being taken to save the MS. These pages were one by one torn out for the printer, and when returned with the proofs were put on the fire. 'I reserved two or three of the leaves, and gave them to the library at Trinity College, Cambridge.'[1]

At about this period, when writing to

---

[1] *Tennyson's Life*, vol. i.

The Life of

Laurence of Tennyson, he says: 'I want to see him again; if you see him, tell him that he must write me a line. Remind him of our dinners and quarrels at the Mitre, Greenwich, etc. Ask him if he will go to Blenheim with me.'

A year or so after this he gave Laurence a commission to paint a portrait of Tennyson, and says, 'I long for my old Alfred's portrait. Mind and paint him quickly when he comes to town, looking full at you.' Again to Laurence, 'I hear you have painted a very good sketch of A. T. Don't do any more to it; take this advice, you won't get the man to sit again easily.' When Laurence finished his work, Fitz-Gerald thought it the best portrait of Tennyson 'at his best time, with a Johnsonian look in it somehow.' Some time after Tennyson's marriage, Fitz-Gerald lent this portrait to Mrs. Tennyson, and with her it remained until he went to Little Grange, where it occupied a prominent position on the walls.

Edward Fitz-Gerald

In 1876, however, he presented it to Mrs. Tennyson, not because he was tired of it, but because he thought it the best portrait of his friend he had seen. To Laurence he says, 'I have returned the portrait to Mrs. Tennyson; for though Tennyson and his son would fain have had me keep it while I lived, I gathered that she missed it from the bedroom where it had once hung. If I had known of that before, I should of course have sent it to her sooner. Now that she is ill and much confined to her room, I would not detain it an hour. So it is gone.'

If Fitz-Gerald was anxious to get into the company of Tennyson, the poet was no less delighted with the companionship of 'Old Fitz.' In those early days Tennyson made a trip to Switzerland with Edward Moxon; and after his return, he lost no time in writing to Fitz-Gerald, describing some of the beautiful spots he had visited and the scenes which had charmed him.

The Life of

He addressed him as 'My dear Fitz,' or 'Dear old Fitz'; and after the publication of the 'Princess,' he wrote:—

'Ain't I a beast for not answering you before? A pint of pale ale and a chop are things yearned after not achievable except by way of lunch. However, this night I have sent an excuse to Mrs. Procter, and here I am alone, and wish you were with me.—Ever yours,   A. TENNYSON.'

The opinions of the two friends on theological questions were strongly in accord. They were liberals in theology, when upholders of this kind of liberalism were less numerous than they are now. The man who penned the lines—

> 'There lives more faith in honest doubt,
> Believe me, than in half the creeds,'

was a long way removed from implicit belief in the summaries of many of the churches. Tennyson dreaded the dogmatism of sects. Like Fitz-Gerald, he had a horror of the doctrine of eternal torment,

Edward Fitz-Gerald

and by this liberalism he was known the world over. When Bishop Colenso was in England in 1865, a party was got up at Oxford to meet him, to which Tennyson was invited, but could not attend. The Bishop, expressing his regret, remarked that he was one man he much wished to see, as he thought he was doing more than any other man to frame the church of the future.

During one of his roaming expeditions in 1840, Fitz-Gerald wandered as far as Leamington, and there accidentally met Tennyson. The two friends had some very pleasant excursions together, going to the grand old castle of Kenilworth, which they found in a ruinous condition, and then to Warwick, where they were delighted by seeing so many quaint old houses, and some of the best architectural groups to be found in England. They visited the castle, and climbed the picturesque Guy's Tower, to have a good view of the surrounding country.

The next day they made their way to Stratford-on-Avon, examined Shakespeare's house, and went into the room in which it is said the great dramatist was born. Every part of this room was scribbled over with names, English and American, peer and peasant. Tennyson, in a fit of enthusiasm, wrote his, though he felt a little ashamed of it afterwards; but he said 'the feeling was genuine at the time, and I did homage with the rest.'

In the summer of the following year Fitz-Gerald paid another visit to Naseby, enjoying himself for three or four weeks by having friendly chats with the farmers, whilst he consumed a quantity of tobacco. He took long walks over the fields and made himself well acquainted with the spot on which the battle of Naseby was fought. This over, his indolent habits had full play for a time. Apathy succeeded activity, and he declared that Naples would not please him more than Naseby.

Edward Fitz-Gerald

This fit of apathy extended longer than usual, and he writes, 'I am afraid I have behaved badly to Thackeray; he asked me to go to Ireland with him, and I have scarce any reason to give why I should not, except one which he would not understand. At present, however, I refuse.' Later still, 'Spedding asks me to Cumberland, and I have no reason but laziness for not going. But I have been to Ireland and done my duty of locomotion for a whole year. I have earned my release from the packing and unpacking of portmanteau till this time twelvemonths.' This reluctance to move is all the more strange, as not many weeks had passed since he had expressed a wish 'to go snipe-shooting with that literary shot James Spedding.'

I have mentioned that another of Fitz-Gerald's College chums, John Allen, the future Archdeacon of Salop, had settled in London. Here was another attraction for an evening when he spent a few days in

The Life of

the metropolis. Allen was a remarkable man. He left Cambridge in 1832, was soon after appointed mathematical lecturer at King's College, London, and in 1833 was ordained chaplain to the College. So great was his reputation among those who had seen his work, that when he was only twenty-six years of age the Bishop of Chichester nominated him as his examining chaplain. In 1839 the Committee of Council of Education selected him as their first clerical Inspector of Schools, and seven years later he was made Archdeacon of Salop. Such was the career of him of whom Fitz-Gerald wrote, 'I owe more to Allen than to all others put together.' Bishop Lonsdale said of him, 'I have never known any man who feared God more and man less than Archdeacon Allen.' He united a strong sense of justice and personal responsibility with a disregard of conventionalism.

Allen was full of zeal for the Church of

Edward Fitz-Gerald

England, but so liberal in his theology that he was always ready to work with men whose views were different from his own. He heard Edward Irving preach when he was astonishing the religious world of London, and for this notable man he ever retained great admiration and sincere respect; he tenderly loved Frederick Demson Maurice, and became acquainted with Archdeacon (afterwards Cardinal) Manning, whose friendship, opposite as were their careers, he retained to the end. Allen was original and quaint, and had a unique simplicity and love of humour. These traits were so much in accord with Fitz-Gerald's opinions and feelings, that the two men soon became close friends; and when Fitz-Gerald heard of Allen as Inspector of Schools, either rebuking a bishop or humiliating a peer, he exclaimed, 'John Allen, I rejoice in you.' He commissioned Laurence the artist to paint a portrait of Allen in order that he might hang it in his room, and thus have his face always to look at.

Allen married in 1834. His marriage was a very happy one. In his wife he found a real helpmate. That he needed somebody to look after him is evident from the fact that he lost the carpet bag containing his wedding garments when he went to be married, and at Bristol had to buy linen and dressing apparatus as well as some cloth for a pair of trousers, which were made for him the next day.

Soon after the marriage, Fitz-Gerald wrote to him thus :—

'Come, I don't believe that your marriage will make any great difference in you after all; and when I meet you, I shall not be able to offend you by many loose and foolish things that I am accustomed to scatter about heedlessly when I meet you with others. I always repent me of having done so, but the joy of meeting you puts me into that tiptop merriment that makes me sin. If

Edward Fitz-Gerald

I only loved you half as well, my conversation would be blameless to you. But you forgive me, and it is always sad to me to think that I shall never be able to sin and repent again in that fashion.'[1]

The year 1842 was memorable to Fitz-Gerald as that in which he made the acquaintance of Thomas Carlyle. It was not, like most of his long friendships, begun in his youthful days, and moreover, it was begun under disadvantages. Fitz-Gerald was not drawn to Chelsea through admiration of the man or his writings; on the contrary, he spoke and wrote disparagingly of those works of Carlyle which he had read. *The French Revolution* came in for his condemnation, and *Heroes and Hero Worship* he described as a perfectly insane book. Two or three evenings spent in gossip about the battle of Naseby, drinking tea and smoking Carlyle's tobacco, dissipated

[1] Grier's *Life of Archdeacon Allen.*

this prejudice, and the two men eventually became fast friends.

Carlyle was at this period engaged on his *Letters of Cromwell*; and when preparing his sketch of the battle of Naseby, he, accompanied by Dr. Arnold of Rugby, surveyed the ground on which it was fought. An obelisk, erected in one of the fields to commemorate the battle, induced both to believe that it was placed there to indicate the centre of the battle. The farm which embraced these fields was the property of Fitz-Gerald's father, and the ground was well known to his son. In consequence of this Laurence the artist introduced Fitz-Gerald to Carlyle in order that he might describe the district. Having heard Carlyle read his description of the ground on which the battle was fought, he at once tried to show him that he had either deceived himself, or been misled as to the exact spot on which Royalists and Puritans, in deadly rage, had a hand-to-hand fight over two

Edward Fitz-Gerald

hundred years ago. The Chelsea sage was incredulous, and not disposed to accept tradition against the evidence of his own eyes. Fitz-Gerald offered to go to Naseby and excavate. He did so, and had trenches dug half a mile away from the obelisk at a spot which tradition had always connected with the graves of the slain. An abundance of closely packed remains of human beings was found, some of the bones and teeth were sent to Chelsea, and Carlyle admitted that the evidence was against him.

Carlyle was so pleased with Fitz-Gerald's earnest endeavour to set him right on this subject, and with the success which crowned his self-imposed labours, the cost of which he offered to share, that he was always glad to welcome the eccentric genius of Woodbridge to his fireside. For a long time after this date, whenever Fitz-Gerald made a journey to London, he never failed to call at Carlyle's for a cup of tea and a smoke, the tobacco being usually enjoyed under an old pear-tree in the Chelsea garden. Sometimes they adjourned to a room at the top of the house, where they sat with the window open smoking and discussing till near midnight. Carlyle's stern dictum that man's business in this world is not to seek for happiness, but to stand where he is placed, and do his duty there, won Fitz-Gerald's cordial sympathy, and each learned to recognise what was sterling and magnanimous in the other's nature.

In the summer of 1843 Fitz-Gerald paid another visit to his uncle in Ireland, arriving in Dublin on a very hot day in the middle of July. The heat made him uncomfortable, and he ordered a warm bath at the hotel. In a short time the waiter informed him that it was ready, the water being heated to 90°. Judge his dismay when he found it scalding hot, and that, to crown his vexation, he had blundered by allowing the man to lock him up in the room instead of his locking the waiter out!

Edward Fitz-Gerald

After a week or two he went to stay with his brother Peter, who some ten years before had married a sister of his Aunt Purcell, and lived on a farm about three miles from his uncle's estate, the farm being managed by a steward. Whilst there he formed one of a picnic party to a place called Pool a Phoka—or the leap of the Golden Horse. This was about nine miles distant; and the party, being rather numerous, travelled on horseback and in carriages, and at the end of the journey were regaled with a plentiful supply of cold veal-pies, champagne, etc. The beauty of the scenery was more to Fitz-Gerald's taste than veal-pie. The water came leaping and roaring through the clefts in the rock, thus forming the head of the river Liffy, into which the company dabbled, and splashed each other, the sun being hot enough to roast them.

Fitz-Gerald wrote for his cousins at Halverstown a prologue to one of Calderon's plays, and they used it for some private theatricals in their own house. He left a good impression behind him in Ireland, and the cousin who wrote me says 'he was a charming person, though a bit eccentric.'

His journeys to London were still frequent, though he wrote that whilst there he 'was sometimes nearly grilled' by the heat. Frederick Tennyson, one of Fitz-Gerald's best correspondents and very dear friends, wrote, after being in Italy many years, that he was coming to England, and wanted to meet him in London. Fitz-Gerald responded that he would be there at the time named, and pig in a garret for two months, in order that they might go to picture sales and buy bad pictures, though he had scarce any money left. This Frederick, a man of considerable ability, was Alfred Tennyson's eldest brother; he took honours at Cambridge, among them the chancellor's medal. Like Fitz-Gerald, he was a great lover of music, and very eccentric. He lived near

Edward Fitz-Gerald

Florence, in a fine villa planned by Michael Angelo, and report says that he indulged his musical taste by 'sitting in his large hall in the midst of forty fiddlers.'

Always anxious to aid Laurence, he obtained for him a commission to paint a portrait of his brother-in-law, the Rev. J. B. Wilkinson of Holbrook. When completed, he wrote, 'The portrait of Wilkinson is capital, and gives my sister and all her neighbours great satisfaction. Mrs. Fitz-Gerald desired a copy of her son-in-law's portrait, and E. F. G. told Laurence that the copy must be slight and conventional. I am not insisting on what is *right*, but on what will, I know, only satisfy the person for whom you do the copy.'

In 1847 he obtained another commission, and wrote to Laurence urging him to come to Woodbridge, as Miss Barton was anxious to have a portrait of her father. This had been talked of for some time; and as Bernard Barton was now sixty-three years

The Life of

of age, and an ailing man, further delay was not desirable. Fitz-Gerald gave his artist friend particular instructions how to travel from London either by steamboat or railway, promising to pick him up at Ipswich, and drive him to Woodbridge by the aid of the washerwoman's pony, where they would sup off toasted cheese and porter with his friend Churchyard. 'Once at Woodbridge,' he added, 'you will see all the faded tapestry of a country town life. London jokes worn threadbare; third-rate accomplishments infinitely prized; scandal removed from dukes and duchesses to the parson, the banker, the commissioner of excise, and the attorney.' The charge for the portrait, a crayon, was fifteen pounds, which sum Fitz-Gerald promptly remitted, expressing at the same time his indebtedness to the artist for the trouble he had taken. It is a good likeness, and was lithographed to form a frontispiece to *Selections from the Poems and Letters of Bernard Barton.*

Edward Fitz-Gerald

PERSONAL CHARACTERISTICS

As the subject of my story had peculiar and distinctive qualities, reference to personal characteristics is essential to the thorough understanding of the man. Our description of his appearance is drawn from recollections of him after he was sixty years of age, and when he began to stoop; but even then he was in height above the medium, and gave the impression of having been a fine, good-looking man in his younger days. He had a melancholy cast of countenance—a mist of despondent sadness hung over his face; a complexion bronzed by exposure to sun and sea air, large nose, deep upper lip, sunken, pale blue eyes and bushy eyebrows, large, firmly closed mouth, dimpled chin, and fine head. About his half-bald head was a comely grace, whilst the fringe of hair on the outskirts was touched by a softened grey, which helped to add to the dignity of his appearance. The expression was severe, that of a man whom you could hardly expect a child to question as to the time of day. Generally he had a dreamy look. His voice, though soft and gentle, was not musical; his manner generally was placid and mild; but when walking along road or street, he was so absorbed in thought, that if addressed, he would answer in a querulous, impatient tone, as though annoyed by impertinent interruption. Once when walking on the Melton Road, he was met by a well-known Nonconformist minister of Woodbridge, who greeted him with 'Good morning, Mr. Fitz-Gerald.' Looking up, he replied, 'I don't know you,' and passed on without further remark, a peremptory dismissal, with no pretence to courtesy. In this he did himself injustice; for if he discovered that the passer-by was

Edward Fitz-Gerald

a person whom he had at the moment failed to recognise, his manner suddenly changed, and he became agreeable and polite. Still, the interruption was not acceptable, and he appeared more anxious to close than to continue the conversation. Customarily his manner was that of a well-bred gentleman, and sometimes the politeness of courtesy even in rebuke was striking. That he could also rebuke in an epigram, when he thought it necessary, is shown by an anecdote given in the *Recollections of Aubrey De Vere* (I quote from the *Daily News*). The author says: ' Here is a story of Lord Tennyson's old and valued friend, Edward Fitz-Gerald :—

' After a large evening party, when nearly all the guests had departed, the rest remained to smoke. In that party was a man celebrated for his passion for titles. On this occasion he exceeded himself. All his talk was of the rich and great, " Yesterday, when I was riding with my friend the Duke of ——." "On Tuesday last the Marquis of —— remarked to me." It went on for a long time; the party listened, some amused, some bored. Edward Fitz-Gerald was the first to rise. He lighted a candle, passed out of the room, stood still with the lock of the door in his hand, and looked back. He could change his countenance into anything he pleased. It had then exchanged in a moment its merry look for one of profound, nay hopeless, dejection. Slowly and sadly he spoke: "I once knew a lord too, but he is dead." Slowly, sadly, he withdrew, closing the door amid a roar of laughter.'

He was extremely careless as to his personal appearance, never knowing when to cast off an 'old acquaintance,' as he described it, in the shape of hat, coat, or shoes. In texture his clothes resembled that worn by pilots, and presented the appearance of being crumpled and untidy. They were put on anyhow, and made to fit him, he used to say, like a sack. Though so meanly clad, plenty of good apparel was found in

Edward Fitz-Gerald

his wardrobe after his decease. In walking he slouched awkwardly, always taking the least frequented footpath. He generally carried a stick, very rarely using an umbrella. In cold or wet weather he wore a large grey plaid shawl round his neck and shoulders. His trousers, which were short, by the aid of low shoes exhibited either white or grey stockings. Perhaps the most noticeable part of his apparel during his later years was an old battered black-banded tall hat, the greasy look of which indicated long service. Worn on the back of his head, this gave completeness to his careless and Bohemian costume. He generally wore a stand-up collar, after the style of Mr. Gladstone, with a black silk scarf carelessly tied in a bow, and he had in addition a white shirt front unstarched, which did not suggest recent acquaintance with the ironing-board.

The Rev. George Crabbe of Merton Rectory (where Fitz-Gerald died), describing his conversation as having been most amusing, says he never seemed happy or light-hearted. 'As a boy, I was rather afraid of him; he seemed a proud and very punctilious man.'

Miss Crabbe, now the only surviving member of the Crabbe family, who had known him from her earliest years, writes me: 'I think we all stood in awe of him, and my impression was that he was a proud man; and like many proud people, didn't mind at all doing things that many people wouldn't do—such as carrying his boots to be mended. We were all very fond of him, and he was always very kind to us as children. I have never forgotten my pride when he admired my garden, all grown over with nasturtiums, his favourite flower (his love of bright colours was extreme), particularly as it had been rather laughed at. I felt he was a friend from that day. He always defended the weakest, and was sure to take their part. We children

Edward Fitz-Gerald

were proud if he let any of us do anything for him, or if we were allowed by our father or sister to go and call him into lunch; but he was sure not to come if called, though he would come if *not* called.

'By my father's wish he used to come in and out just as if it was his own house. He translated most of his Persian poems sitting under one of the trees in our garden. I have the table we, or he, used to carry out. How delighted we were whenever he came, and how we missed him when he was away! He seemed a part of our life, he was so kind and thoughtful for us.

'Mr. Fitz-Gerald was full of fun, but his moods varied a good deal. We children delighted to hear him talk. In those days we only listened. My father or brother or eldest sister talked, but we enjoyed it. He was peculiar, but that he liked to be; a perfect gentleman, and very noble-looking, he couldn't do a mean thing.

'On reading his letters to Mrs. Kemble,

I could recall having heard him say nearly every word in them. He used to talk of her, of his friends Thackeray, Tennyson, and all the rest. It was delightful to hear him talk about them, and how fond of them he was. He would say "dear old" whoever it was he talked of. . . . My impressions of Mr. Fitz-Gerald are that he was extremely honourable—one you could entirely trust, truthful, proud, a fund of wit in him, and could set any one down completely if they were at all pushing; faithful to old friends, difficult to please.'

Charlotte Brontë was so nervous and shy, that it was irksome to her to be introduced to strangers. She paid a visit to Mrs. Gaskell, expecting to find the family alone; but to her surprise, a lady friend sat at table with them. This created a nervous tremor, a shiver ran over her, and she was unusually silent all the evening. She was fond of music, and whilst staying with Mrs. Gaskell two musical ladies invited her to give them

Edward Fitz-Gerald

a call next day, when they would sing to her. She accepted the invitation, but on reaching the house her courage failed. Mrs. Gaskell was with her, and they walked up and down the street for some time, but it was of no use; at last her friend had to make the call, and to offer the best apology she could for the non-appearance of Miss Brontë.

The feeling thus manifested by the author of *Jane Eyre* will illustrate the effects of nervousness from which Fitz-Gerald suffered, for he was equally shy in his way.

After the circulation in America of a few copies of his *Translations*, his fame spread rapidly among the scholars in that country; and Professor Goodwin, of the University of Boston, when on a visit to England, was anxious to spend a few hours with the translator. He wrote to Fitz-Gerald proposing to visit him at Woodbridge; but Fitz-Gerald replied that he could not bear the thought of his coming all that way for such a purpose. The proposal actually worried him. This looks like a morbid sense of humility, but it was natural to the man.

In March 1882 a lady residing in Woodbridge intimated that she meant to pay Mr. Fitz-Gerald a visit of congratulation on the seventy-third anniversary of his birth, which was close at hand, whereupon he begged her to stay at home, and neither say nor write anything about it!

This shyness, or self-disparagement, or reserve, which may be looked upon as one of the eccentricities of genius, in some instances operated prejudicially to himself. If he was in the presence of persons, as he thought, not in sympathy with him, he was either silent or uncomfortable. This, of course, left an unfavourable impression on the minds of strangers. He was once invited to a small dinner-party to meet Macready; but when there, he was nearly silent. He looked upon the eminent tragedian as the lion of the evening, and

Edward Fitz-Gerald

kept aloof from him, as he did not like celebrities.

The lives of other eminent men furnish similar examples. Tennyson was extremely shy and sensitive. Rogers once had his hand on Dr. Johnson's knocker, but lacked the courage to use it, and ran away without seeing the author of the *Lives of the Poets.* The poet Gray was always striving to be elegant in person and dress, but was as much of a recluse, and just as silent in a mixed company as Fitz-Gerald. Steele says that Addison, when with friends, was delightful in conversation; yet Pope tells us that before strangers he preserved his dignity by a stiff silence, and describing Gay, said he was in wit a man, in simplicity a child, and this would do for Fitz-Gerald also.

Writing to Frederick Tennyson in 1850, he said, 'I get shyer and shyer even of those I know'; and when his old friend, Fanny Kemble, arrived in London,

The Life of

after living in America some years, with whom he had exchanged letters monthly for a long period, he went up to see her. The next day she had a letter saying, 'I should very gladly have "crushed a cup of tea" with you last evening, coming prepared so to do, but you had friends, and so I went to the pit of the Old Haymarket Theatre.'

Another characteristic was his hatred of London. He had no hesitation as to the comparative merits of life in London and life in the country. 'London is hateful to me. I long to spread wing and fly into the clear air of the country.' He felt sure that the great city was a deadly plague, worse than the disease so called that came to ravage it, 'and the fresh cold and wet of our clay-fields is better than fog that stinks *per se.*'

It was not merely London that he hated. Londoners came in for a share of his dislike. 'The men and women were,' he said, 'all clever, composed, satirical, selfish, and well

Edward Fitz-Gerald

dressed. One finds but few *serious* men in London. I mean serious even in fun, with a true purpose and character, whatsoever it may be. London melts away all individuality into a common lump of cleverness.' He hated nothing so much as that superficial cleverness which is so common in towns, and held 'that the dulness of country life is better than the impudence of Londoners.'

He lamented the false estimate of respectability that prevailed in society, and the assumption that only certain kinds of employment were genteel. 'Such things as wealth, rank, and what is called respectability I don't care a straw about.' As may be supposed, he escaped all anxiety in connection with tailors, and scorned the fine clothes in which some of his neighbours, to whom the accident of suddenly acquired wealth constituted their only social distinction, decked themselves. Against the tyranny of custom he resolutely set himself.

Like Charles Lamb, he never greatly cared for the society of what are called good people. He had discovered that in what is spoken of as good society there was plenty of visiting, but no communion. In evening parties the association of ladies was self-evident, but the interchange of thought was disregarded. He found more real enjoyment in the fisherman's cottage than in the home of the squire, where he said awful formalities stifled the genuine flow of nature. He preferred the society of his books to that of most of his wealthy neighbours, and was impatient of idle talk. Compliments were intolerable to him; even thanks for gifts he thought would have been better withheld.

From his dislike of London and London society it will be supposed that he was strongly attached to country life, and the supposition is perfectly true. For him nature abounded with charms, and the rusticity of the fields filled his heart with joy. A band

Edward Fitz-Gerald

of reapers or mowers delighted him; the sound of the whetstone, as it slipped over the blade of the scythe, was music in his ears. His love of nature is frequently shown in his letters. He appeared to feel a personal companionship with birds. In spring and summer evenings he sat with open window smoking whilst the blackbirds and thrushes rustled to roost, and the nightingale had the field to himself. Speaking of the blackbird and the nightingale, he says, 'I have always loved the first best, as being so jolly, and the note so proper from that golden bill of his.' He dearly remembered—

> 'The robin that chirped in the frosty December,
> The blackbird that whistles through flower-crowned June.'

His garden was frequently tenanted in the winter by a blackbird. During a hard winter he kept one alive by providing a saucer of bread-and-milk for it every day; and at the beginning of the next winter he was pleased to hear a blackbird's notes, the same calls, and as far as he could tell, the same bird, come to look for his food-supply.

Though looking so grave, Fitz-Gerald was often a very different man from what his gravity would lead one to suspect. He had a keen sense of humour; there was sharpness in his wit, pungency in his satire, but these were guarded by great discretion and good nature; yet he sometimes did not hesitate to fire humorous shots at grave subjects, but this was done with such delicacy as to render it easy to detect the wisdom which underlay the humour.

To collect examples of this side of Fitz-Gerald's character is difficult, for his friends do not seem to have stored them in memory. One of the most intimate of his Woodbridge friends says, 'It would be difficult for me to quote instances.' Another says, 'He was full of fun, always saying things in the driest way; not laughing himself, but his expression was humorous.' Not every sage has a Boswell!

Edward Fitz-Gerald

The examples of Fitz-Gerald's fun, which I have heard recited, fail to give a full idea of the man who named his little yacht *The Scandal*, because he thought defamation travelled faster than anything else in Woodbridge.

Fitz-Gerald and Captain Brooke were nearly of the same age, had spent the greater part of their lives within a few miles of each other's homes, and greatly enjoyed each other's company. Fitz-Gerald said his Ufford friend was 'Frank by name, and frank by nature.' Like himself, Mr. Brooke was a good linguist. He wrote and spoke with facility several languages, and as great book-lovers they had much in common, but in habits and dress were far apart. The smart, prim, and even youthful aspect of the one contrasted strongly with the careless and slovenly appearance of the other.

A remark which Fitz-Gerald one day made to Captain Brooke was worthy of Charles Lamb. Leaving with a friend the

The Life of

railway platform at Woodbridge, Fitz-Gerald saw, in the station-yard, Captain Brooke mounted on his high-mettled charger. After the ordinary greetings had passed, he exclaimed as he was walking off, 'Brooke, you should be ashamed of yourself.'—'What for?' asked the Captain.—'Because you falsify your years; you've no business to look so young.' The force of these words will be appreciated by all who recollect the care with which the good-natured Squire of Ufford arrayed himself in all his glory with the aid of tailor and valet.

Fanny Kemble, in one of her articles in the *Atlantic Monthly*, notes a characteristic of Edward Fitz-Gerald, who remained her friend throughout life. She says he was an admirable scholar and writer, who, if he had not shunned notoriety as sedulously as most people seek it, would have achieved a foremost place among the eminent literary men of his day. But with all his rare intellectual and artistic gifts, 'he led a

Edward Fitz-Gerald

curious life of almost entire estrangement from society, preferring the companionship of rough sailors and fishermen to that of lettered folk.'

And Mr. Edward Clodd says: 'In the district in which Edward Fitz-Gerald was born, and lived, and died, reminiscences of the man whom the yokels in their usual assessment of genius called "dotty" are yet plentiful. How could they appreciate the man who hobnobbed with all; whose large-heartedness took the oddest and drollest of ways; who hearing that a poor tradeswoman was in trouble, emptied her shop of all its feminine wares at West End prices; who stood port wine to the fisher-folk when they sighed for a quart of beer; who helped them to buy their boats and gear, and never asked for the repayment of the loans; who shared ventures with them in herring craft —*Meum et Tuum* one of these was named, only there was more *tuum* than *meum*, because he paid the losses and refused the gains—how could these bumpkins know that here was a man, the peer of more famous contemporaries? . . . The prophet met the usual fate in his own country, but yokels are not the only mortals to whom truth of perspective is denied.'[1]

A characteristic which all may admire was his generosity. He was generous to a fault, and one of the least worldly-minded men that can be imagined. He would not give a subscription or donation for publication. He followed the precept, 'Let not thy left hand know what thy right hand doeth,' but that he did give largely has been gratefully remembered by many of his poorer neighbours. The reviewer of his works in *The Quarterly*, who, I believe, was an intimate friend, says, 'We can imagine it to be very possible that he never gave a guinea to a charitable society in his life, but very certain that he gave a great many to unfortunate individuals with whom he came in contact.'

[1] Pilgrimage to Fitz-Gerald's Grave.

Edward Fitz-Gerald

Soon after the Rev. C. B. Ratcliffe was appointed to the Vicarage of St. John's, Woodbridge, he called upon Fitz-Gerald, as one of his wealthy parishioners. Fitz-Gerald declined to see him, but sent word, 'If Mr. Ratcliffe wants money for any one in his parish, and writes to me, he shall have it.'

In answer to my inquiries, the rev. gentleman kindly wrote: 'My personal acquaintance with Edward Fitz-Gerald was very slight. He was living in the strictest retirement when I came to St. John's in the latter part of 1881; if I remember rightly, his nieces were staying with him when I first called, and I gathered from them that with the exception of intimate friends he saw no one. I received a £5 note from him soon afterwards, and another the next year for distribution among the poor of the parish, accompanied by a letter to the effect that *no word of thanks was to be offered to him.*'

Miss Crabbe, writing on the same subject, says: 'He was wonderfully generous, but never talked about it, not only helping the poor, but giving hundreds to those who could not make a living by their work as artists, etc., or buying their pictures. He spent nothing on himself, unless it was in the purchase of a good painting.'

A gentleman who was on intimate terms with him for some years writes: 'He had his old pensioners, as he called them, to whom he allowed something weekly, monthly, or quarterly, and he would ask two or three ladies to disburse money for him at Christmas, or for sickness or deserving cases. He lent money in more than one case to help persons in business at a nominal rate of interest, after a time making them a present of the entire amount by putting the note of hand in the fire.'

He had an antipathy for female beggars, especially when in the guise of district visitors. Some of these, he said, assumed a monopoly of religious truth, obtruded themselves into the poor man's home, for

Edward Fitz-Gerald

the purpose of probing his conscience and taking the measure of his creed. He associated all these with Dickens's Mrs. Jellaby, and treated them accordingly. Two young ladies of the religio-philanthropic turn called upon him, and sent in the message that they wanted a shilling towards getting a cot for an invalid child. He sent out his answer: 'Tell them to go home and mend their stockings.'

By will he directed his executors to reward handsomely, at their discretion, all persons 'who may be in my service at the time of my decease, or who have attended or waited upon me during my last illness.' Whilst living at Little Grange, he had an aged couple—Mr. and Mrs. How—to take charge of his household. To these he left an annuity of seventy pounds a year for their joint lives, and for the life of the survivor. And it is pleasant to see how he kindly remembered in his will the daughters of the dearest of his friends.

The Life of

His utter disregard for wealth, and his willingness to make a heavy sacrifice for the public good, are well illustrated in a letter he wrote just prior to the breaking out of the Crimean War. He says: 'I am told that if war comes, I may lose some £5000 in Russian bankruptcy, but I can truly say I would give that and more to ensure peace and goodwill among men at this time.'

As an illustration of the Good Samaritan spirit which filled the heart of Fitz-Gerald, I add the following:—He became acquainted with a clerk in a London office, who belonged to friends living in Suffolk, and who had the misfortune to combine small means with very delicate health. Having resolved in his own mind that pure air was the one thing needful for this young man, Fitz-Gerald determined to get him to Woodbridge to rusticate whenever he could be spared, and for several years the bank holidays, with some additional days, were made use of for this purpose. On these

Edward Fitz-Gerald

occasions they sailed daily down the Deben to Bawdsey, or went to Aldeburgh, where they dashed about in sail-boats on the open sea, drinking in all the oxygen they could inhale. The young man is living, married, and comfortably settled, and owes much to Fitz-Gerald for his considerate thoughtfulness.

Another case was that of an artist in London, whom he knew only through a Suffolk friend who had passed away. He was poor, original, independent in spirit, and lived in a garret, which he would not allow to be cleaned. One morning Fitz-Gerald received from him a note, written in pencil, from which the recipient judged that the poor fellow was very ill. He immediately wrote to his friend Laurence, the artist, to ascertain if the object of his solicitude had all that, in his sad condition, he really *wanted* or wished for. By the same post he also wrote to the landlord begging similar information. To Laurence he said:

'I know not what his means are, and I should wish to supply what is wanted at such a time. Mr. R—— is a delicate and proud man, and has always refused any offer I made him. His small means have been equal to his very small wants while he was in health, I dare say; but I know not how it may be now.'

Three days after writing thus, he sent two brace of pheasants to Mr. Laurence, asking him to have *one* of the birds cooked and sent cold to the invalid, with the words, 'I do not think you will mind this little trouble for a poor artist.' Later on Fitz-Gerald went twice to London to see the poor fellow, who was thought to be sinking, but strength was only gradually failing. As the few pounds he had saved had now dwindled to nothing even with the help he had received, Fitz-Gerald and two others clubbed together to maintain him for the rest of his life, and thus remove from his mind an oppressive load of anxiety. After his second visit to

Edward Fitz-Gerald

the invalid, he wrote to Laurence, 'I believe he has really been better since his landlady sent him up a plate of good meat for his daily dinner.' By whose considerate thoughtfulness this was supplied may readily be judged.

These incidents help to show what a kind heart beat under the slatternly attire with which Fitz-Gerald was content; but it is difficult to do justice to this side of his character, for the simple reason that, as I have said, his many acts of tenderness cannot be traced. If any think that his brusqueness was harsh and unfeeling, they will, I hope, set off one feature against the other, and probably conclude that his benevolence more than compensated for his apparent austerity.

I close this chapter by laying before my readers a copy of a letter which Lord Tennyson has kindly permitted me to take from his charming biography of his father. It is from Fitz-Gerald to Alfred Tennyson after their joint visit to James Spedding's

The Life of

home in Cumberland in 1835. At that time Tennyson's income was small; but he, noble-minded man, lived a life of self-denial, and worked on, determined to perfect his poems before he offered a second volume to the public. The delicate tenderness which Fitz-Gerald breathes in this letter, whilst offering pecuniary aid to his friend in what he thought his hour of need, reflects credit on his head and heart, and does more than would pages of description to show the real spirit of the man :—

'LONDON, *July 2nd*, 1835.

'DEAR TENNYSON,—I suppose you have heard of the death of James Spedding's sister-in-law; for my part, I only came to know of it a day or two ago, having till then lived out of communication with any one who was likely to know of such things. After leaving you at Ambleside, I stayed a fortnight at Manchester, and then went to Warwick, where I lived a king for a month.

Edward Fitz-Gerald

Warwickshire is a noble shire; and the spring being so late, I had the benefit of it through most of the month of June. I sometimes wished for you, for I think you would have liked it well. . . . I have heard you sometimes say that you are bound by the want of such and such a sum, and I vow to the Lord that I could not have a greater pleasure than transferring it to you on such occasions; I should not dare to say such a thing to a small man, but you are not a small man assuredly; and even if you do not make use of my offer, you will not be offended, but put it to the right account. It is very difficult to persuade people in this world that one can part with a bank-note without a pang. It is one of the most simple things I have ever done to talk thus to you, I believe; but here is an end, and be charitable to me.'—(Vol. i. page 155.)

The Life of

HIS LITERARY WORK

ONE of Fitz-Gerald's most intimate friends said that the first half of his life was passed in quiet reading and thinking; he might have added in roaming about, making discreet journeys in uneventful directions. His letters to his friends at that time give little evidence of a desire for literary work, although they often enlighten them by his independent criticism, which at once exhibits good scholarship and keen perception. His reading was extensive, and he easily digested what he read, and thus continually kept adding to his stores of knowledge. A reviewer has remarked that Fitz-Gerald was highly endowed, but in the absence of spur to action 'he was content to let the sword of his intellect rust in the scabbard.'

Edward Fitz-Gerald

Almost all his friends were connected with literature, and he must have been conscious of his ability to take part in the world of letters; but he confesses that, at this period of his life, indolence was his besetting sin, whilst his extraordinary diffidence restrained him from testing his powers. Much that was published struck him as not rising above mediocrity; and his belief that 'unless a man can do better, he had best not do at all,' kept him from trying to rival his friends; even late in life he spoke of some of his small escapades in print as nice little things which may interest a few people for a few years, but he felt somewhat ashamed 'of having allowed his leisure to drive him into print when so many much more capable people keep silent.' With such feelings, it is not surprising that he was more than forty years of age before he published anything that would place him among the list of authors.

When preparing the three-volume edition

The Life of

of his friend's *Letters and Literary Remains*, Mr. Aldis Wright made a discovery which seems to prove that Fitz-Gerald did make some attempts at authorship during the years in which he is supposed to have been idle. Whilst examining a *Common Place Book* belonging to Archdeacon Allen, he saw a poem entitled 'The Meadows in Spring,' bearing the initials E. F. G., and the date Naseby, Spring 1831. This he identified as the poem which Fitz-Gerald had told him he wrote when little more than a lad and sent to the *Athenæum*. The date of its appearance in that journal is July 9, 1831.

No mention is made in the published *Letters* of this poem, and the mystery which hangs about its publication marks strongly the eccentricity of its author. It is a typical illustration of those peculiarities by which more than one member of the Fitz-Gerald family gained notoriety. Although sent to the above-named journal in June or July,

Edward Fitz-Gerald

it had, strange to say, been published in the preceding April in Hone's *Year Book* with a letter from the author. Its second appearance naturally excited surprise among literary men; and Charles Lamb wrote to a friend telling him that the *Athenæum* had 'been *hoaxed* with some exquisite poetry that was two or three months ago in Hone's *Year Book*. I do not know who wrote it, but 'tis a poem I envy.' The copy here given is from the latter source.

THE MEADOWS IN SPRING

 'Tis a sad sight
  To see the year dying;
When autumn's last wind
  Sets the yellow woods sighing,
   Sighing, oh sighing!

When such a time cometh,
  I do retire
Into an old room,
  Beside a bright fire;
   Oh! pile a bright fire!

The Life of

And there I sit
   Reading old things,
Of knights and ladies,
   While the wind sings;
     Oh! drearily sings!

I never look out,
   Nor attend to the blast;
For all to be seen
   Is the leaves falling fast;
     Falling, falling!

But, close at the hearth,
   Like a cricket sit I;
Reading of summer
   And chivalry;
     Gallant chivalry!

Then with an old friend,
   I talk of our youth;
How 'twas gladsome, but often
   Foolish, forsooth,
     But gladsome, gladsome!

Or, to get merry,
   We sing an old rhyme
That made the wood ring again
   In summer-time;
     Sweet summer-time!

Edward Fitz-Gerald

Then take we to smoking,
  Silent and snug;
Nought passes between us,
  Save a brown jug;
    Sometimes! Sometimes!

And sometimes a tear
  Will rise in each eye,
Seeing the two old friends,
  So merrily;
    So merrily!

And ere we to bed,
  Go we, go we,
Down by the ashes,
  We kneel on the knee;
    Praying, praying;

Thus then live I,
  Till breaking the gloom
Of winter, the bold sun
  Is with me in the room;
    Shining, shining!

Then the clouds part,
  Swallows soaring between;
The spring is awake,
  And the meadows are green.

The Life of

I jump up like mad;
 Break the old pipe in twain,
And away to the meadows,
 The meadows again!
Epsilon.

The poem was accompanied by the following letter to the editor:—

'These verses are in the old style, rather homely in expression, but I honestly profess to stick more to the simplicity of the old poets than the moderns, and to love the philosophical good-humour of our old writers more than the sickly melancholy of the Byronian wits. If my verses be not good, they are good-humoured, and that is something.'

When sent to the *Athenæum*, the author wrote the editor: 'My verses are certainly not in the present fashion. . . . If they are fitted for your paper, you are welcome to them.' The editor replied: 'They are fitted for any paper . . . they are deep in feeling and sweet in harmony. We have a suspicion that we could name the writer; if so, we are

Edward Fitz-Gerald

sure his name would grace our pages as much as his verses.' From this it has been conjectured that the editor had in his eye Charles Lamb.

The flattering testimony of so acute a critic as Charles Lamb to the poetical power of 'The Meadows in Spring,' when he declared, ''Tis a poem I envy,' and the strong commendation which the editor of the *Athenæum* appended to the poem in his columns, would have stimulated most young aspirants to poetic fame to make greater efforts. But the singing impulse did not last with Fitz-Gerald. There was nothing in his surroundings to impel him to write; he was sure to ask, What good will it do? This hesitancy kept him in chains. Fame did not disturb him, and what he said of his sister Lusia was applicable to himself at this period of his life, 'She wishes to exert herself, which is the highest wish a Fitz-Gerald can form.' He delighted in Epicurean ease, and con-

The Life of

tended that, having no capacity for achievement, he had a right to take his ease as a privileged onlooker.

That he had the ability to command attention as a poet, notwithstanding all his disclaimers, is evidenced by his poem, 'Bredfield Hall,' printed and circulated among his friends in 1839. He said of Omar's quatrains 'that they had the ring of the true metal,' and these verses on his birthplace are not less worthy of being so described. The version here given is from a MS. copy in the possession of an intimate friend, and bears the latest revision of the author. It differs slightly from the copy printed by Fitz-Gerald's editor, and it is greatly improved by the use of the eight-line stanza.

BREDFIELD HALL

Lo, an English mansion founded
In the elder James's reign,
Quaint and stately, and surrounded
With a pastoral domain.

Edward Fitz-Gerald

With well-timbered lawn and gardens,
 And with many a pleasant mead,
Skirted by the lofty coverts,
 Where the hare and pheasant feed.

Flank'd it is with goodly stables,
 Shelter'd by coeval trees;
So it lifts its honest gables
 Tow'rd the distant German Seas.
Where it once discerned the smoke
 Of old sea-battles far away;
And victorious Nelson's topmasts,
 Anchoring in Hollesley Bay.

O'er the meadows that surround it
 Broods the dusk of days gone by;
O'er the solemn woods that bound it,
 Ancient sunsets seem to die.
Through the cypress in the garden
 Sighs the warning voice of old;
One same cuckoo calls afar off,
 One same crocus breaks the mould.

But whatever storm might riot,
 Cannon roar, and trumpet ring;
Still amid these meadows quiet
 Did the yearly violet spring.
Still heaven's starry hand suspended
 That light balance of the dew;
That each night on earth descended,
 And each morning rose anew.

The Life of

And the ancient house stood rearing,
  Undisturb'd her chimneys high;
And her gilded vanes still veering
  Toward each quarter of the sky.
While like wave to wave succeeding,
  Through the world of joy and strife,
Household after household speeding,
  Handed on the torch of life.

First, Sir Knight in ruff and doublet,
  Arm in arm with stately dame;
Then the cavaliers indignant
  For their Monarch brought to shame.
Languid beauties limn'd by Lely,
  Full-wigg'd Justice of Queen Anne,
Tory squires who tippled freely,
  And the modern Gentleman.

Here they lived, and here they greeted,
  Maids and matrons, sons and sires,
Wandering in its walks, or seated
  Round its hospitable fires.
Oft their silken dresses floated,
  Gleaming through the pleasure-ground;
Oft dash'd by the scarlet-coated
  Hunter, horse, and dappled hound.

Till the bell that not in vain
  Had summon'd them to weekly prayer,
Called them one by one again
  To the church—and left them there!

Edward Fitz-Gerald

They with all their loves and passions,
    Compliment, and song, and jest,
Politics, and sports, and fashions,
    Merged in everlasting rest!

So they pass—while thou, old Mansion,
    Markest with unaltered face
How like the foliage of thy summers
    Race of man succeeds to race.
To most thou stand'st a record sad,
    But all the sunshine of the year
Could not make thine aspect glad
    To one whose youth is buried here.

In thine ancient rooms and gardens,
    Buried—and his own no more
Than the youth of those old owners,
    Dead two centuries before.
Still though 'scaping Time's more savage
    Handiwork this pile appears,
It has not escaped the ravage
    Of the undermining years.

And though each succeeding master,
    Grumbling at the cost to pay,
Did with coat of paint and plaster
    Hide the wrinkles of decay;
Yet the secret worm ne'er ceases,
    Nor the mouse behind the wall;
Heart of oak will come to pieces,
    And farewell to Bredfield Hall!

The Life of

The above was issued in 1839, and twelve years elapsed before *Euphranor, a Dialogue on Youth*, was published. This, the first book that Fitz-Gerald issued, is a small volume of eighty-one pages, without preface or dedication. It is a Platonic dialogue in academic style, with a framework of landscape in which the colleges, the halls, and the river at Cambridge are introduced. Students and townsmen are assembled on the banks of the Cam to watch the efforts of the several crews in a University boat-race. Mr. Edmund Gosse says of this book: 'Slight perhaps, and notably unambitious, *Euphranor* could scarcely have been written by any one but Fitz-Gerald, unless possibly in certain moods by Landor, and it remains the most complete and sustained of his prose works.'

Of this book Alfred Tennyson declared that the description of the University boat-race was one of the most beautiful fragments of English prose extant. I give the passage entire as quoted by Mr. Gosse :—

Edward Fitz-Gerald

'Townsmen and Gownsmen, with the tassell'd Fellow-Commoner sprinkled here and there, Reading Men and Sporting Men, Fellows and even Masters of Colleges not indifferent to the prowess of their respective crews,—all these conversing on all sorts of topics, from the slang in *Bell's Life* to the last new German revelation, and moving in ever-changing groups down the shore of the river, at whose farther bend was a little knot of ladies gathered upon a green knoll faced and illuminated by the beams of the setting sun. Beyond which point was at length heard some indistinct shouting, which gradually increased, until "They are off—they are coming!" suspended other conversation among ourselves; and suddenly the head of the first boat turned the corner; and then another close upon it; and then a third; the crews, pulling with all their might, compacted into a perfect rhythm; and the crowd on shore turning round to follow along with them, waving hats and caps, and cheering " Bravo, St. John's!" "Go it, Trinity!" the high crest and blowing forelock of Phidippus' mare, and he himself shouting encouragement to his crew, conspicuous over all, until the boats reaching us, we also were caught up in the returning tide of spectators, and hurried back toward the goal; where we arrived just in time to see the ensign of Trinity lowered from its pride of place, and the eagle of St. John's soaring there instead. Then, waiting a little while to hear how the winner had won and the loser lost, and watching Phidippus engaged in eager conversation with his defeated brethren, I took Euphranor and Lexilogus under either arm (Lycion having got into better company elsewhere) and walked home with them across the meadow leading to the town, whither the dusky troops of gownsmen with all their confused voices seemed as it were evaporating in the twilight, while a nightingale began to

Edward Fitz-Gerald

be heard among the flowering chestnuts of Jesus.'[1]

In the following year (1852) he published another volume, still anonymous—*Polonius*, a collection of 'Wise Saws and Modern Instances,' from Bacon, Selden, Carlyle, Newman, and others. This was the last of his prose efforts in volume form. He now began the labours on which in the literary world his fame rests, that of a translator of poetry; but in after years he contributed some local articles to a Suffolk magazine, from which I shall quote.

Fitz-Gerald had a great love for the Suffolk dialect, and Major Moor's *Suffolk Words and Phrases* was one of his favourite books. So strong was his interest on this subject, that he made considerable collections towards a new edition, and for years he meditated giving the fruit of his labours to the public. His want of resolution came

[1] *Fortnightly Review*, July 1889.

The Life of

in the way, and the idea was abandoned. This was a loss to literature, as he was just the man for the work.

Fortunately, another collection of his was almost entirely preserved. From his love for the sea sprang a strong attachment to sailors and beachmen, whose acquaintance he strove to make at Aldeburgh, at Dunwich, and at Lowestoft. When among them he amused himself by picking up phrases which were habitually on their tongue. These he was induced to contribute to the pages of the *East Anglian*, an archæological journal published in 1868 by Mr. S. Tymms of Lowestoft, under the title, 'Sea Words and Phrases along the Suffolk Coast,' and with them he incorporated some of his Suffolk dialect. This collection will be found in vols. iii. and iv. of *East Anglian*, old series, and covers twenty-six pages. His letter to the editor, and a few examples from the collection, are given as follows:—

Edward Fitz-Gerald

'SEA WORDS AND PHRASES ALONG THE SUFFOLK COAST

'*To the Editor of the "East Anglian."*

'MY DEAR SIR,—You have asked me to send you some of the Sea Phrases I have picked up along our Suffolk Coast—from Yarmouth to Harwich—and here they are.

'Certainly, the only two *East Anglian* Vocabularies we had till within the last two years were deficient in this respect; and a considerable deficiency one must reckon it, considering how much of the country whose phraseology they undertake to register is sea-board. But Major Moor, though born at Alderton, only two miles from the waves, went out to India as soon as he was in his teens; and when at length returned to settle in England, occupied himself with an inland, though not far inland, farm, for the remainder of his wise, beneficent, and delightful life. Forby was busy with a parish near Downham Market; and though both might, under certain conditions, have almost heard the sea that washes their coasts, they neglected the language of its people for that of those "whose talk is of bullocks."

'I had for some time meditated a fusion of their two Glossaries, taking the more accurate Forby for groundwork, to be illustrated with Major Moor's delightful Suffolk humour, and adding the Sea Phrases in which they both were wanting. Two years ago, however, Mr. Nall in some measure anticipated my dread exploit by the very good East Anglian Vocabulary which he appended to his *Yarmouth Guide*; bringing to his task a great deal of etymological research, such as the march of philology has made much easier since Forby's time, but such as I could make no pretensions to. I had, however, been more among the sailors, if not among the philo-

Edward Fitz-Gerald

logists, than Mr. Nall; and being very glad of his book, sent him the words I now send you, to be incorporated, if he saw good, in any future edition of his book. He thanked me courteously, and since then I have heard no more of him.

'Meanwhile, you think these words of mine may find a proper niche in your *East Anglian,* and you are very welcome to them. Picked up idly, with little care how or whence they came to hand, I doubt they will make a sorry show in your grave pages, whether as regards quantity or quality. They may, however, amuse some of your readers, and perhaps interest others in guessing at their history. On the whole, I think if you print them as I send them, it must be in some Christmas number, a season when even antiquaries grow young, scholars unbend, and grave men are content to let others trifle. Even *Notes and Queries,* with all the scholars that Bruce so long has led, sometimes smile, sometimes doze, and

The Life of

usually gossip about what is the fashion to call Folklore (of which I send you some also) at Christmas.—And so, wishing you, at any rate, a happy one, I remain, yours very sincerely, E. F. G.

'*P.S.*—I add a little incidental gossip at the end, in order to make up one number all of a piece, if you think your subscribers won't drop off in consequence.'

'MITTEN. "Dead as a Mitten"—that is the sea phrase. Another article as well appreciated by the Seaman is commonly used for the same comparison ashore. A gamekeeper near Lowestoft was describing how some dignitary of the Church—he knew not what—was shooting with his master. Some game—I know not what—was sprung; and the gamekeeper, at a loss for any correct definition of his man, called out, " Blaze away, your Holiness!" and blowed if he didn't "knock it over as dead as a Biscuit!"

'HEART OF THE WIND. The strength that

Edward Fitz-Gerald

promises endurance. A less determined wind has no '*Weight*' in it; no *Heart*, a very comfortable apathy, by the bye, in a North-easter, unless to those who are running away from it. "A hard-hearted wind for ye, Master!" will be sung out by some one going before it, as he passes some wind-bound captain looking disconsolately over his ship's quarter.

Before I leave the word, I will add a Suffolk superlative of which it is "the heart," almost as good as any of Major Moor's. It was said to me by one honest Guernsey of another, to whom I owe the greatest part of this Sea-slang, "*He's the best-heartedest Fellow that ever I knew.*"

'BARK. "The surf *bark* from the Nor'ard"; or, as was otherwise said to me, "The sea ain't lost his voice from the Nor'ard yet," a sign, by the way, that the wind is to come from that quarter.

'A poetical word such as those whose business is with the sea are apt to use.

The Life of

Listening one night to the sea some way inland, a sailor said to me, "Yes, Sir, the sea roar for the loss of the wind," which a landsman properly interpreted as only meaning that the sea made itself heard when the wind had subsided.

'BETTY. To be over nice in putting things to order. "He go betty, betty, bettyin' about the boat like an old woman."

'BOTTOM'S OUT. The bottom of the sea, when beyond reach of the lead.

'FAIR. Clouds running to. "Do you think the wind 'll hold?" "Lord bless ye, look at the clouds a runnin' to a fair like."

'HOLIDAY. Any interval which the tarrer of a vessel has neglected to cover. "Jem have left plenty of holidays, anyhow."

'FEETS. Feet; the *s* intensitive added to the end instead of the beginning, I suppose. "She was feets and feets under water by the time we got to her." The Irish footman did not go so deep when he

Edward Fitz-Gerald

announced to the Drawing-room, "Mrs. Foote and the Misses Feet!"

'SOLDIER. A red herring; or the remaining tobacco in a pipe. "I say, just wait till I've smoked this soldier out."'

In 1877-78 the *Ipswich Journal* set aside a column or two weekly for the insertion of 'Suffolk Notes and Queries,' and Fitz-Gerald added to the interest of the collection by occasionally sending a contribution. His Notes, which are not numerous, are all signed 'Effigy,' a play upon his initials, E. F. G.'

His *Letters* excepted, there is but little more to say of his prose writings. In 1849 he penned a charming Biographical Sketch of his friend Bernard Barton, which was prefixed to the subscription edition of *Selections* from the works of that poet, and a few years later he contributed to the *Gentleman's Magazine* a lengthy obituary notice of the Rev. George Crabbe of Bredfield. Every now and then he proposed doing something to benefit literature, but his vacillation was so great that he seldom made a start. His 'Readings from Crabbe' were printed, but never published. Of this small work he wrote to a friend: 'My book is all printed, unless a preface has to be added, which I dislike doing; above all, I will *not* if my friends Spedding, Wright, etc., decide that it may as well remain *unpublished*. I know that publishers will do very little for Crabbe, and still less for me, more kicks than halfpence from reviewers, etc. I shall not be at all sorry to have only spent my time and money on a little work which I think will please my friends.' After his death a large number of copies were found in a trunk in the lumber-room.

It has been said of Richardson's *Clarissa* that nothing short of breaking a leg, and being laid up a couple of months in a dull house, would make it possible to read through that remarkable novel. Fitz-

Edward Fitz-Gerald

Gerald would remedy this by pruning the pedantry of the tale, and the remainder would be, he said, one of the great original works in the world of fiction. He prepared an abridgment, but left it for his executors to consign to the lumber-room or to the fire.

The last and best of Fitz-Gerald's prose works—his inimitable *Letters*—remain to be noticed. They were written on the spur of the moment to amuse or interest a friend, with whom he was anxious to have a light-hearted chat on paper, when talk was not to be had. Had the translation of Omar brought no fame, these gems of English literature would in all probability never have been heard of, whilst it is now certain they will be the delight of thousands of readers who will not trouble themselves about the ideas and sentiments in the quatrains of the Persian philosopher.

In these easy and familiar letters you see at once the best side of the man—cheerful, kindly, human. Their frankness, their simple confidence in friendly intercourse, the way in which he unbosoms himself, unconsciously exhibiting his queer ways and whims, are among their greatest charms. They are models of honesty, many are as transparent as a child's prattle. Their purity and freedom from conventionalism are striking features. The reader, before he has covered half a dozen pages, will realise that the writer never contemplated publication. Gray's *Letters* are recognised as models of epistolary art, but they are fastidious and precise, and indicate preparation and polish. Fitz-Gerald's, on the other hand, are spontaneous and careless to a degree, and bear the strongest signs of being intended only for the eye of the friends to whom they were addressed. 'That his letters to his friends were to constitute a prized record of his uneventful existence, he was millions of miles from surmising. Their unconsciousness of merit is, indeed,

Edward Fitz-Gerald

one of the many ingredients in the charm exercised by them. No *ingenue* in white muslin was ever more innocent of design to make an effect. Yet their excellence, as mere products of the writing art, is unmistakable. Scarcely a sentence falls flat, or rings false, yet there is no suspicion of "preciosity." To Fitz-Gerald's broad common-sense nothing would have seemed more contemptible than the affectations and far-fetched expedients by which some modern stylists in verse or prose attempt to capture distinction.'[1]

It must not be forgotten that Fitz-Gerald's correspondents ranked among the most eminent literary men of England and America, and one may be sure that to such he could write nothing dull. He had good taste in music and the fine arts, and a keen sensibility as to what was true or false in literature. On these subjects, his sly hits, delicate satire, and racy but honest criticism,

[1] *Edinburgh Review*, October 1894.

must prove attractive to all who can enjoy the best specimens of English letter-writing. Autobiographical glimpses are continually given in his artless way; he speaks of his occupations day by day; his correspondents could see the man he was in these confiding allusions to the passing hour. In short, they had before them, not only the man, but his mode of life, and could foretell with fair accuracy his movements, if not his hopes and fears of the near future.

Edward Fitz-Gerald

HIS SPANISH AND PERSIAN TRANSLATIONS

It would be difficult to name the exact date at which Fitz-Gerald commenced the study of Spanish literature; but it was probably about 1850, when he was visiting Professor Cowell at Bramford, near Ipswich. Many years afterwards, he said, 'All that I know of Spanish was taught me by Cowell; he was always the teacher, and I the pupil.' The suggestion that he should learn it was a very fortunate one, as the study not only opened up a new world of interest, but, what was better, was the means of awakening in Fitz-Gerald the conviction that the translation of poems ought to be the future labour of his life. He became a great admirer of Calderon's plays, said that all Calderon's had something beautiful in them, and in 1853 published a free translation of six of his dramas. This was the only book to which Fitz-Gerald was ever tempted to affix his name. The volume is now very scarce, as, in consequence of an unfavourable critique in the *Leader*, and a 'more determined spit at me' in the *Athenæum*, Fitz-Gerald speedily withdrew it from circulation. He felt assured that the translation of Calderon's *Six Dramas* was on the whole well done and entertaining, yet he fully expected that the London Press would condemn it on the ground that it was too free.

Nothing daunted, he very soon commenced the translation of what has always been considered the finest of Calderon's plays, *The Wonder-Working Magician*. But it was put aside; and when he knew that Professor Cowell was about to return to England, he recast his translation, and printed a few copies for private circulation. An able reviewer has remarked that, with

Edward Fitz-Gerald

all its shortcomings, this play of Calderon's will always excite and sustain a high degree of interest, and it may be characterised as the high-water mark of religious and philosophical inquiry within the limits of *Romanism*.

Its apparently sceptical character probably induced Shelley to give to the world a translation of this drama, but the complaint against his version was that it was more a free paraphrase than an accurate translation. It is very likely that the same kind of influence operated on Fitz-Gerald, as he found that the author's views in this play coincided in many ways with his own agnostic perceptions. He was convinced that the problems which have occupied the minds of the greatest intellects in all ages are one and the same—the contest between humanity and the eternal powers of the universe.

Mr. Owen, author of the *Five Great Sceptical Dramas of History*, says: 'The dramas that have most impressed the minds of men have been dramas whose subjects and characters have pertained to sceptical freethought. Thus the greatest of Greek plays is without doubt the *Prometheus* of Æschylus; the noblest of Hebrew books, with a dramatic plot and character, is the *Book of Job*; the greatest play of England's greatest dramatist is the *Hamlet* of Shakespeare; the noblest drama of modern poets is the *Faust* of Goethe; and the same problem which has been taken by Calderon, for consideration from a Roman Catholic point of view, is the finest of his dramas.'

Fitz-Gerald's great admiration for Æschylus, whom he called the Raffaelle of tragedy, and his intense love of Shakespeare, whose *Hamlet* he thought should be read rather than acted, are well known to all who are familiar with his correspondence. He was anxious to make the *Wonder-Working Magician* well known to philosophical students, and of his masterly translation it was said that his version reads like an original

Edward Fitz-Gerald

composition of the best days of the English language. His modest estimate of his own intellectual powers received a rude shock when, in 1882, a letter arrived from the Spanish Ambassador, announcing that the Calderon Medal had been awarded to him for the beauty of his translations from the Spanish dramatist.

Fitz-Gerald's acquaintance with Spanish literature was almost exclusively confined to its fiction, and after the translation of the *Wonder-Working Magician* very little is heard of his Spanish studies. He was, however, so fascinated by *Don Quixote*, when he read it in the original language, that he said it was worth learning Spanish to enjoy its beauties. He loved the very dictionary in which he had to hunt up the words he wanted. This love for the Spanish Don remained with him to the end of his life. When yachting he always had *Don Quixote* on board as a companion.

Professor Cowell, who had drawn his

attention to Persian as well as Spanish, succeeded in inoculating him with a strong desire to acquire a thorough knowledge of that language. The Professor was well aware of the strength of his friend's powers, and felt assured that if he once mastered the language he would not be satisfied until he had translated some of the best Persian works for the benefit of English readers. Fitz-Gerald always deferred to the judgment of the Oriental scholar; and when a new poem was named, said he would wait until the Professor had read it and was able to recommend it for translation.

In 1853 he began to amuse himself by the study of Persian, his friend being his guide; and Fitz-Gerald was pleased to think that master and pupil had a subject in which a common interest enabled them to study together. He was very quick in acquiring the rudiments of a language; and with the help of Jones's *Grammar*, and Eastwick's *Gulistan*, he had the year after

Edward Fitz-Gerald

translated an allegory by Jami called *Salaman and Absal*, though he feared that he had stilted the Persian's ingenious prattle into Miltonic verse. He also translated, but did not print, an abridgment in verse of some of Attar's stories, which he thought better than Jami's, and he was attracted by Hafiz; but all these were put aside when he became well acquainted with the MSS. at Oxford, the translation of which was to make his name famous throughout the civilised world. At this, the very commencement of his Persian labours, he was anxious to rub off as little as possible of the Oriental colour of the work, but he felt that to be successful the translator must recast the original more or less into his own likeness.

The 'Rubáiyát' of Omar Khayyám, which has now obtained a world-wide reputation, was, at the time of Fitz-Gerald's translation, almost unknown among the English-speaking public. Professor Cowell, whilst looking

The Life of

over a mass of uncatalogued Oriental MSS. of Sir William Ousely's in the Bodleian Library, accidentally came upon the most beautiful Persian MS. he had ever seen. Written on thick yellow paper, with purple black ink, profusely powdered with gold, the attention of the Sanscrit scholar was immediately arrested, and on examination he found that this was an original MS. of a poem by Omar Khayyám. He had not previously seen anything by the same author; and the poem, being comparatively free from coarseness and ignoble illustrations, which so often disfigure Persian authors, was a great attraction to him. Pleased with it himself, it was not long before he recommended it to the notice of Fitz-Gerald, who at once went to the Bodleian and examined with him the hitherto unknown treasure, Fitz-Gerald immediately recognising its beauty. This was in 1856. In the same year the Professor made a transcript of the MS. for his own and Fitz-Gerald's use; and

Edward Fitz-Gerald

the latter was so charmed with the poem, that for a considerable time the MS. was his constant companion.

When visiting his friend Browne at Bedford in June 1857, he read scarcely anything else; and afterwards, at Geldeston Hall, he might be seen studying Omar at an open window. The result of this continued application was that in a short time he thoroughly discerned the character of the poem, and acknowledged that he preferred it to the work of any Persian that he had seen. Omar's philosophy, he said, is one that never fails in the world. 'To-day is ours,' etc. He told his friend Cowell, 'You see all his beauty, but you don't feel *with* him in some respects as I do.' 'Old Omar's poem rings like true metal.' He afterwards remarked that Omar sang in an acceptable way what the generality of men felt in their hearts, but had not found expressed by any poet.

It is time to inquire who was this Omar, whose work as a poetic philosopher has won

The Life of

for him in a few years an enduring name and a large circle of admirers. What can be gathered relating to his life may be briefly stated.

In the latter half of the eleventh century there lived in Persia an astronomer known as Omar, who bore in addition the poetical name of Khayyám, which signifies a tent-maker. He was born at Naishápúr, a city in the province of Khorassan, bordered on one side by a mountain range, surrounded by fertile fields and watercourses, and girded by gardens which had an abundance of fruit and flowers. It is not certain what was the ethnic origin of the man, whether his extraction was Arab or Iranian, but from his name it is conjectured that he belonged to the hereditary guild of tentmakers.

As may be imagined, few facts can be obtained respecting the early period of his life. Tradition says that he left his birthplace and travelled so as to sit at the feet of one of the greatest of the wise men of

Edward Fitz-Gerald

Khorassan. Of this man it was the universal belief that every boy who read the Koran, gained knowledge, or studied the traditions under his instructions, would win the favour of fortune. Be this as it may, he became celebrated in algebra; and studied the sciences, more especially astronomy, to such good purpose, than when he went to Merv his reputation made him a favourite at Court, and he was one of the eight learned men engaged to revise the old Persian Calendar. It is evident that Omar was a man of learning and genius; but his scientific work, if not wholly obscure, is not distinguishable in the early annals of astronomy.

Omar was not an ambitious man. He loved the retirement of home and the opportunity to study rather than the authority of official position. When he returned to Naishápúr, the Vizier, a friend of his boyhood, obtained for him the offer of a Government appointment; but this he declined, saying, 'The greatest good you can

The Life of

confer on me is to let me live in a corner under the shadow of your fortune, to spread wide the advantages of science, and pray for your long life and prosperity. The Vizier was so pleased by the sincerity shown by this refusal, that he permitted him to live in a garden house in the suburbs of his native town, and granted him an annual pension from the treasury in order that he might devote himself to study. By this means he became unrivalled in science, and the paragon of his age. He died a natural death about 1123 at Naishápúr, his old age being untroubled.

The Calcutta MS. gives a story of Omar's latter days, which, as Mr. Murray remarks, is exquisitely fit and gracious, as it shows that humility and the love of nature remained with him to the end of his life. The facts are given by one of his pupils, who says: 'I often used to hold conversation with my teacher Omar Khayyám in a garden; and one day he said to me, "My tomb shall

Edward Fitz-Gerald

be in a spot where the north wind may scatter roses over it."' Years after, when this pupil went to see the grave, he found it just outside a garden, and trees stretched their boughs over the wall, dropping their flowers upon his tomb.

Omar's Epicurean audacity of thought and speech caused him to be regarded askance in his own time and country. He is said to have been especially hated and dreaded by the Sufis, whose practice he ridiculed, and whose faith amounted to little more than his own when stripped of the mysticism and formal recognition of Islamism, under which Omar would not hide. For this, or some other reason, this poet has never been popular in his own country, and his MSS. have been scantily transmitted abroad. Still, it must be admitted to be a singular thing that such a heterodox and seemingly unprofitable poem should have survived without the aid of the printing-press through the havoc of seven stormy centuries,

The Life of

during which Persia and Khorassan have been scourged by fire and sword, and the frail life of manuscripts must have been in constant danger. The outspoken heterodoxy of the Rubáiyát also must have rendered Omar's writings especially liable to the hostile pursuit of Moslem priests.[1]

The position of Omar among Orientalists is peculiar. In many respects he contradicts preconceived notions of Oriental character. Among philosophers his attainments in science are at the present day unknown, but his fame rests on his poetry, which still holds its individuality. Von Hammer speaks of him as one of the most notable of Persian poets. He was master of his own language in its best days. A large number of quatrains current under his name are undoubtedly spurious, and some of the best Persian scholars declare that Omar's may be known by their quality, viz. simplicity of language, perfection in rhythm, and

[1] *Macmillan's Magazine*, Nov. 1887.

Edward Fitz-Gerald

epigrammatic completeness. He did not favour the world with narrative poetry, but occupied himself with the problems of life and death, sin and fate, and embodied his interpretations in a series of quatrains, a peculiar form of four-lined verse, sometimes all rhyming, but oftener the third line a blank, thus, from first and fourth editions :—

> 'Awake! for morning in the Bowl of Night
> Has flung the stone that puts the stars to flight;
> And lo! the Hunter of the East has caught
> The Sultan's Turret in a Noose of Light.
> .   .   .   .   .   .
> 'I sometimes think that never blows so red
> The Rose as where some buried Cæsar bled;
> That every Hyacinth the Garden wears,
> Dropt in her Lap from some once lovely Head.'

It is to be observed that there is no coherence in Omar's work. His quatrains are arranged in a purely meaningless and arbitrary alphabetical order. Here is the epigram of a scoffer, there the ejaculation of a pious inquirer; while the carol of a wine-bibber is followed by a stanza of tender love.

The Life of

It has been said that he is the sole representative of the age of freethought in Persia; whilst a competent judge has declared that his Rubáiyát is a compound of the Sunnite teaching which he enjoyed in early life, and of the contempt of religion characteristic of the age in which he lived.

The leading ideas of the Rubáiyát are pleasure, death, and fate, and his predominant states of mind are the sensuous and the rebellious. Wine is the favourite theme; indeed, one gets wearied with the constant recurrence of its praise, and with exhortations to drink, but we must remember that drinking had in the East at that time no vulgar associations. Of pleasure he says:—

> 'Life void of wine, and minstrels with their lutes,
> And the soft murmurs of Iranian flutes,
> Were nothing worth; I scan the world and see,
> Save pleasure, life yields only bitter fruits.'

One of his disciples has remarked that to an age to which the darkest side of alcohol has been revealed, the poetry which began

Edward Fitz-Gerald

and ended with 'wine, and wine, and wine,' may seem so far as it goes to jar with spiritual ideals; but leaving aside narrower considerations, Omar appeals to much that is highest in the aspiration of the human soul, and the appeals are couched in deep-toned, searching language.

To comprehend this man of genius and learning, whose work stands out so prominently in the midst of the conventional poetry of Persia, the time in which he lived must be considered. It was the period of the first crusade. The orthodox creed of the early Moslem Arabs was cooling down into culture and cant. The Persians had not accepted it, and their old Zoroastrian creed yielded slowly before the fierce persuasions of the Crescent.

Can we be surprised that the work of such an author, who is acknowledged to be an unparalleled figure in the usually conventional literature of the East, should be an attraction to Edward Fitz-Gerald?

The Life of

What has been described as the irreligious tone of Omar's Rubáiyát would not be likely to repel his translator, as he himself had drifted a long way from orthodoxy. Some Persian scholars consider that Omar, though not orthodox, was more of a doubter than a disbeliever, and this was Fitz-Gerald's position. Dr. Thompson, the Master of Trinity College, writing to a friend, said, 'One of the finest living men among my intimates, Edward Fitz-Gerald, was prisoner in Doubting Castle the last half of his life.' In fact, the poetic philosopher and his translator were twin spirits walking the earth seven hundred years apart. Omar said, 'We are helpless—thou hast made us what we are'; and Fitz-Gerald desired that if any text was put upon his tombstone, it should be this: 'It is he that hath made us, and not we ourselves,' identical in idea, though not in words.

I have said that many of Omar's quatrains

Edward Fitz-Gerald

ridicule current creeds and systems, but these were saturated with the priestcraft of the age. He was most tender to the dumb life of the world around him, and he finely said that it was 'better to be touched by God's pure light within a tavern, than be in darkness within His temple.' And again, 'Dogmas admit only what is obliging to the Deity, but refuse not thy bit of bread to another, guard thy tongue from speaking evil, and seek not the injury of any being, and then I undertake on my own account to promise thee Paradise.' Of Creeds he wrote :—:

> 'Although the Creeds number seventy-and-three,
> I hold with none but that of loving thee.'

A careful study of Omar convinced Fitz-Gerald of the value of the Rubáiyát, and so embued his poetic mind with enthusiasm for the author, that he resolved to translate him in a way that would make the words of the poet almost his own :—

The Life of

'Vex not to-day with wonder which were best,
 The Student, Scholar, Singer of the West,
 Or Student, Scholar, Singer of the East,
 The Soul of Omar burned in Edward's breast.'

The resolution to execute this translation in a way worthy of itself soon brought him face to face with various difficulties. His friend Cowell, who had aided him greatly in the study of Persian, was just at this time appointed Professor of History at the Presidency College, Calcutta, and soon afterwards went to India. This was a sad blow to Fitz-Gerald, who, being naturally indolent, needed the stimulus to regular work which his more industrious friend was able to give, and for a time he seemed to have lost his right hand. But the absence of Mr. Cowell brought its compensations; it fortunately led to his writing to him by every mail, explaining his progress and his difficulties, and the replies were encouraging. He had Cowell's copy of the Bodleian MSS. of Omar Khayyám in his possession, and not many

Edward Fitz-Gerald

months elapsed before the professor sent him a copy of the Omar MS. in the Asiatic Society's Library at Calcutta. To perfect himself in Persian, whilst staying with his brother Peter at Twickenham, he made a copy of Professor Cowell's transcript from the Bodleian MSS., and sent it to a volatile Frenchman, Garcin de Tassy, 'in return for courtesies received.'

When the discovery was made at the Bodleian, it was thought that the writings of Omar were very scarce; but though they are known to be rare, it is now admitted that there are in existence nearly twelve hundred stanzas,[1] which are ascribed to the Persian philosopher. Not more than a third of these are believed to be genuine, and the MSS. are widely distributed. There is no copy at the India House, none at the Bibliothèque Nationale at Paris. Only one is known in England, No. 140 of the Ouseley MSS. at the Bodleian, written at

[1] *Macmillan's Magazine.*

Shiroz A.D. 1460. This contains but 158 Rubáiyát. One in the Asiatic Society's Library at Calcutta contains 516, though these are swollen to that number by all kinds of repetition and corruption. Von Hammer speaks of his copy as containing about 200, while Dr. Sprenger catalogues the Lucknow MS. at double that number. Professor Cowell, whilst in India, met with a copy of a very rare edition printed at Calcutta in 1836. This contains 438 Tetrastichs, with an appendix containing others not found in some MSS.

Fitz-Gerald had copies of the Bodleian and the Calcutta MSS., as well as the Paris edition by M. Nicolas, to examine, and he soon found that the first part of his task was selection. This he set about with great diligence, promptly recognising his vocation as a translator. As a translator and more. For he worked 'on the theory that translation must be paraphrased to be readable, and that to retain forms of verse and

Edward Fitz-Gerald

thought irreconcilable with English language and English ways of thinking was fatal to vitality.'[1] He believed that the philosophy of Omar Khayyám might be woven together from the stray threads scattered throughout the Rubáiyát, although of itself it is fragmentary, and contains no evidence that the quatrains were parts of a consecutive whole. Indeed, it seems more likely that they were 'thrown off at intervals between the wine-cup and the calendar' at various periods, and were collected by some of his disciples after his death.

It is not at all likely that the Rubáiyát in its original form would have pleased the generality of English readers. It is too remote in time and place, too quaint, too detached and jerky. Fitz-Gerald saw this; and though full of humility as to his own powers, he was conscious that he had the faculty of making some things readable which others had left unreadable. He dis-

[1] *Quarterly Review*, Oct. 1894.

played his genius as a translator; and what is so desirable in such a matter, succeeded in producing on his reader the effect of the original. He became interpreter as well as translator. He brought the scattered quatrains together, and aimed to give expression to Omar's philosophy in better proportion than the Persian did for himself. His skill was shown by the manner in which he moulded them into a poem, flexible in form, while preserving the integrity of each stanza. He was wonderfully successful in setting thoughts and phrases from the Persian in English verse, and equally successful in catching their rhythm. Though he has transposed and condensed in what some scholars call a reckless fashion, it is now pretty generally admitted that 'whatever he touched he turned into poetic gold, yet at the same time the gold in another form was in the original,' and he thus laid the work of Omar Khayyám before the English public

Edward Fitz-Gerald

in so attractive a form as to link his name with that of Omar for all time.

The translation completed, the question arose how he could best introduce it to the literary world. *Fraser's Magazine* was at that time one of the best—if not the best—channel for such a purpose. It happened that Mr. Parker, its publisher, had sometime previously asked him to send a contribution. Now that he had finished, to his satisfaction, the translation of a number of Omar's quatrains into English verse, Fitz-Gerald knew that he had a novelty to offer, and having penned a brief introduction, he forwarded the article to Parker. The receipt of the contribution was acknowledged, and it was intimated in addition that the editor had accepted it. Month after month Fitz-Gerald looked in vain for its appearance. The MS. over which he had spent much time and labour reposed quietly in the editor's drawer. Having waited more than twelve months and waited in vain, he became convinced that the editor or publisher was afraid to print the translation, and he thereupon withdrew it and determined to issue it himself. His courage in taking this course is to be commended.

He immediately set about enlarging the work to nearly double its size, by adding a number of quatrains which he had withheld out of regard to the prejudices of the readers of *Fraser*, and he prepared to publish it himself in pamphlet form. One of his reviewers has remarked that now began the 'dismal business of trying to find a publisher bold enough to embark on the perilous enterprise of printing this little book of immortal music called the Rubáiyát of Omar Khayyám.' It does not appear to have been a dismal business to Fitz-Gerald. Beyond sending the magazine article to Parker, there is no evidence that he sought a publisher. In 1850, whilst hunting for old books, he became acquainted with Mr. Bernard Quaritch,

Edward Fitz-Gerald

the well known London bookseller. Business acquaintance ripened into personal friendship. When his version of the Rubáiyát was ready, he had it printed as a small quarto pamphlet of twenty-one pages, with thirteen pages of introduction. He ordered it to be put in brown paper wrappers, withheld his name as author, but used Mr. Quaritch's name as publisher without asking his permission, and fixed the price at Five Shillings! His want of business tact is shown by the way in which he announced its publication. It does not appear to have been advertised in any newspaper or literary periodical, and Mr Quaritch is not aware that copies were sent for review. Its publication was simply made known by the appearance of title and price in Mr. Quaritch's Oriental catalogue! Fitz-Gerald gave copies to a few friends, among them William Bodham Donne, and the eccentric George Borrow. He sent one to Professor Cowell at Calcutta, who, he says, was

The Life of

naturally alarmed at it, 'he being a very religious man'; but his friend Thomas Carlyle was twelve years in finding out that Fitz-Gerald was the translator of Omar. Thus in beggarly disguise as to paper and print and binding appeared that matchless translation of Fitz-Gerald's, of which Tennyson years after wrote—that—

> . . . . . 'Golden Eastern lay,
> Than which I know no version done
> In English more distinctly well.
> A Planet equal to the Sun
>   Which cast it, that large infidel
> Your Omar.'

Around the publication there hangs quite a halo of romance. Mr. Justin Huntly M'Carthy has remarked that the fate of Edward Fitz-Gerald's Omar Khayyám is almost unique in literature. Certainly few books have had so strange a destiny. In the published letters of Fitz-Gerald there is no evidence (a letter from Mr. Ruskin excepted) that it attracted the smallest attention, or in any way brought either

Edward Fitz-Gerald

praise or blame from the outside world. To the admirers of Omar and Fitz-Gerald, it seems marvellous that this magnificent poem, the fame of which is now heard in all the literary circles of Europe and America, should, at the time of its publication, be so dismal a failure as to become a complete drug in the market. The story of this lamentable failure has been given before, but not exactly as Mr. Quaritch told it to me. The real facts I now give mainly in his own words.

In 1859, Edward Fitz-Gerald went to the shop of Mr. Bernard Quaritch in Castle Street, Leicester Square, and dropped a heavy parcel there, saying, 'Quaritch, I make you a present of these books.'

The parcel consisted of nearly two hundred copies of the first edition of the *Rubáiyát of Omar Khayyám*. Mr. Quaritch tried to sell the books, first at half-a-crown, then at a shilling, and again descending he offered them at sixpence, but buyers were not attracted. Then, in despair, he reduced the book to one penny, and put copies into a box outside his door with a ticket, 'all these at one penny each.' At that price the pamphlet moved, in a few weeks the lot was sold, and in this way one of the finest gems of English literature was dispersed among a not over discerning public. It thus appears that had it not been for Mr. Bernard Quaritch's penny box the whole first edition would have remained unsold, and in all probability no more would have been heard of Omar Khayyám, or of Edward Fitz-Gerald in connection with him.

As might be expected, the originally neglected translation in a few years grew greatly in demand. In some ways the reaction was more extreme than the previous neglect. There is a legend floating about that such remarkable men as Dante Gabriel Rossetti, Algernon Charles Swinburne, and Captain Richard Burton, were among those who discovered the hidden treasure in the penny box.

Edward Fitz-Gerald

Mr. Edward Clodd has favoured me with the following note:—

Mr Swinburne told me that a day or two after he bought his copy he returned to the penny box, but found the stock sold out, and Mr George Meredith has often narrated to me how, when awaiting a visit from Mr Swinburne at Esher, he saw the poet approaching and flourishing a brown brochure, which he must fain sit down to read through to his host, despite a cooling luncheon to tempt him to postpone the reading. And an immediate effect of Fitz-Gerald's verses on Mr. Swinburne's mind was the composition of some of the stanzas of *Laus Veneris.*

These men, all of them poets by nature, speedily recognised the genius which these pages displayed—they felt that here was a man who was as much a poet as was Omar himself. They made known the beauty of Fitz-Gerald's version, which gained favour slowly but surely. Each of this trio of poets proclaimed its value among his friends, and through it became devotees of Omar. Being men of culture, whose judgment could be trusted, the disciples of Omar gradually increased, from a small band to a growing army of intellectual men and women.

Yet it was not until 1868 that the demand for a second edition of the translation was sufficient to justify republication. A third was issued in 1872, and a fourth in 1879. These were all issued, well printed, and well bound by Mr. Quaritch at his own expense. That gentleman paid the author a small honorarium for each edition, and Fitz-Gerald gave it away in charity. One of these payments was his contribution to a Persian Famine Fund. These several editions were issued during the life of the translator, but without his name. Each had alterations and additions, by which the number of stanzas was increased. The first edition had seventy-five, the second a hundred and ten.

Edward Fitz-Gerald

The popularity of the book in the United States may be understood from the large number of copies printed, ranging in price from 20 cents to 25 dollars. One of these editions is pre-eminent for the beauty of its printing—old style type, with ornamental head bands in gold and colours. Another was printed in folio, cloth gilt, with fifty-six full page engravings from drawings by Elihu Veddor. One publisher in the State of Maine has, since 1894, issued five editions, each of which numbered a thousand copies. In 1901, when the copyright of the first edition will have run out in England, a host of cheap issues, testifying to the immortality of the poem, will doubtless appear.

In another aspect the reaction has become almost a mania. Among the disciples of Omar a strong desire sprang up to have a copy of Fitz-Gerald's first edition. There was a craving for the brown paper covered pamphlet to be placed with their literary treasures. Mr Huntly M'Carthy, writing in 1889 of the first edition not finding buyers, and being ultimately dispersed at a penny a copy, said, 'The man who could buy these two hundred copies back now at a guinea a copy would be making a magnificent bargain. The last time I saw a copy of the first edition quoted in a bookseller's catalogue it was priced at four guineas, and I do not imagine that it would be easy to get one at that price now.' Until 1898 six pounds was considered a big price at a sale for a copy of the first edition, but now it is worth more than its weight in gold. In February 1898 a copy was offered for sale in Sotheby's Rooms. There was nothing remarkable about it. It was simply an ordinary copy in its original wrapper, and after a very smart competition, the lot was knocked down for £21. The increasing admiration for the translator, and its rarity, sent up its price by leaps and bounds. What seems almost as marvellous as the price is the fact that the book was bought

Edward Fitz-Gerald

for Mr. Quaritch, who, nearly forty years previous, had sold the very same copy for one penny.

No doubt can exist as to Fitz-Gerald's ability as a translator; but regard for his memory, and reverence for his work, induce me to quote a few authorities on the subject.

Professor Charles Eliot Norton, of Harvard University, in the *North American Review*, speaking of Fitz-Gerald and his work, says :—

'He is to be called translator only in default of a better word, one which should express the poetic transfusion of a poetic spirit from one language to another, and the re-representation of the ideas and images of the original in a form not altogether diverse from their own, but perfectly adapted to the new conditions of time, place, custom, and habit of mind in which they reappear. It has all the merit of a remarkable original production, and its excellence is the highest testimony that could be given to the essential impressiveness and worth of the Persian poet. It is the work of a poet: not a copy, but a reproduction; not a translation, but a re-delivery of a poetic inspiration. . . . In its English dress it reads like the latest and freshest expression of the perplexity and of the doubt of the generation to which we ourselves belong.'

Dr. Talcot Williams, the eminent Arabic scholar, remarks: 'In my judgment, Omar owes more to Fitz-Gerald than he does to himself, as far as English readers are concerned. I do not mean by this, that Omar's thoughts differ from the utterances of Fitz-Gerald's translation, but the utterance owes so much in our language to the form in which Fitz-Gerald has cast it.'

His Excellency, the American Ambassador, Colonel John Hay, has kindly permitted me to make use of the address which he delivered to the members and friends of the Omar Khayyám Club in December 1897. He said, 'I can never

Edward Fitz-Gerald

forget my emotions when I first saw Fitz-Gerald's translation of the Quatrains. Keats, in his sublime ode on Chapman's Homer, has described the sensation once for all:—

> "Then felt I like some watcher of the skies,
> When a new planet swims into his ken."

'The exquisite beauty, the faultless, the singular grace of those amazing stanzas, were not more wonderful than the depth and breadth of their profound philosophy, their knowledge of life, their dauntless courage, their serene facing of the ultimate problems of life and of death. Of course the doubt arose, which has assailed many as ignorant as I was of the literature of the East, whether it was the poet or his translator to whom was due this splendid result. Could it be possible that in the Eleventh Century, so far away as Khorassan, so accomplished a man of letters lived, with such distinction, such breadth, such insight, such calm disillusion, such cheerful and jocund despair? My doubt lasted only till I came upon a literal translation of the Rubáiyát, and I saw that not the least remarkable quality of Fitz-Gerald's poem was its fidelity to the original. In short, Omar was an earlier Fitz-Gerald, or Fitz-Gerald was a re-incarnation of Omar.

'It is not to the disadvantage of the later poet that he followed so closely in the footsteps of the earlier. A man of extraordinary genius had appeared in the world, had sung a song of incomparable beauty and power in an environment no longer worthy of him, in a language of a narrow range; for many generations the song was virtually lost; then by a miracle of creation, a poet, a twin brother in spirit to the first, was born, who took up the forgotten poem and sang it anew with all its original melody and force, and all the accumulated refinement of ages of art. It seems to me

Edward Fitz-Gerald

idle to ask which was the greater master, each seemed greater than his work. Omar sung to a half barbarous province; Fitz-Gerald to the world. Wherever English is spoken or read, the Rubáiyát have taken their place as a classic.

'Certainly our poet can never be numbered among the great popular writers of all time. He has told no story. He has never unpacked his heart in public, he has never thrown the reins on the neck of the winged horse, and let his imagination carry him where it listed. But he will hold a place for ever among that limited number, who, like Lucretius and Epicurus, without rage or defiance, even without unbecoming mirth, look deep into the tangled mysteries of things, refuse credence to the absurd and allegiance to arrogant authority, sufficiently conscious of fallibility to be tolerant of all opinions, with a faith too wide for doctrine and a benevolence untrammelled by creed, too wise to be

The Life of

wholly poets, and yet too surely poets to be implacably wise.'

The Right Honble. H. H. Asquith, in his address to the members of the 'Omar Khayyám Club' in April 1898, said: 'You have had many appreciations of Omar from far more capable hands than mine. Nor has he escaped faithful treatment from the critics, who shake their sorrowful heads over his manifold lapses from the path of orthodox belief and correct conduct. A poet who avows that he sampled and rejected the various beliefs which were on exhibition in the market of his day—who tells us that he

. . . . . . "Evermore
Came out by the same door wherein he went,"

bears a perilous resemblance to the agnostic, whom some of us have met. The preacher who exhorts his followers to abandon the wearing pursuit of the secret of life—to sit down and fill their cups with "the old familiar juice," and

Edward Fitz-Gerald

not to "heed the rumble of a distant drum," is not very far from the "stye of Epicurus." Why is it that, from the moment the genius of Fitz-Gerald made him known to all who speak the English language, he had taken rank with the immortals, whom no change of taste or fashion can dethrone? I do not pretend to give a full answer to the question, but there are one or two considerations which are obvious. First, as regards form; apart from the strange fascination of the metre, there is within a narrow compass, in point of actual bulk, a wholeness and completeness in Omar, which belongs only to the highest art. . . . There is nothing in Omar's work that could be added or taken away without injuring its perfection. Then as regards substance, where else in literature has the littleness of man, as contrasted with the trifling infinitude of his environment, the direct result of serenity and acquiescence, been more brilliantly or more powerfully enforced? The "million bubbles that the Eternal Saki pours from his bowl," the clay which is responsive under the treating of the potter, the ball that is thrown hither and thither about the field, the "helpless pawns" that the great player moves into impossible positions with an inscrutable purpose, the endless procession of empty pageantries, the sultans and heroes who are, with all their pomp and pride, after all but passing inmates of the "Father's Caravan-Serai"—such is the crowd of vivid and moving images which Omar's panorama presents to us. As we gaze upon it, the great men who seemed to the intoxicated vision of their own time to be the dominating forces of the world, are seen to be but the flickering notes in the sunbeam, the crest raised by a gust of wind upon the rising and falling wave.

"The wine of life keeps oozing drop by drop,
The leaves of life keep falling one by one."

Edward Fitz-Gerald

'These, if I understand them right, are the thoughts and pictures with which Omar and Fitz-Gerald have permanently enriched the poetry of the world.'

Mr. Swinburne has expressed the wish that 'the soul and spirit' of Omar's thoughts may be tasted in that most exquisite English translation, sovereignly faultless in form and colour of verse, which gives to those ignorant of the East a relish of the treasure, and a delight in the beauty of its wisdom.

Mr. Justin Huntly M'Carthy, in the *Westminster Gazette*, writes:—'An English country gentleman came across the works of a Persian poet, which appeared to him to repay translation, and he certainly would have been greatly surprised if he had been told that forty years later the English-speaking race would cherish with familiar affection the name of a Persian poet, and place the country gentleman's translation among the Classics.'

The Life of

Mr. Edward Clodd says:—[1] 'The themes of the Rubáiyát are perennial. As magnet to the pole, the spirit of man turns to the questions which the ancients asked, to which no answer comes; to which each man must find such solution as he can. The limitations of knowledge which no man's experience can transcend; the silence of the past, the return of none of the great company who have gone behind the veil through which I might not see; the transitoriness of all things;

> " Whether at Naishápúr or Babylon,
>   Whether the cup with sweet or bitter run,
> The wine of Life keeps oozing drop by drop,
>   The leaves of Life keep falling one by one;"

the sympathy these thoughts engender in face of our common frailty and common destiny; the cheeriness, withal, which with other preachers, old and new, bids a man "bend to what he cannot break,"

[1] *A Pilgrimage to the Grave of Edward Fitz-Gerald.* By Edward Clodd. (Privately printed for the Members of the Omar Khayyám Club, 1894.)

Edward Fitz-Gerald

"rejoice in his youth," "take the cash and let the credit go," and refuse nought that ministers to life's completeness; are they not written in the *Rubáiyát* of Omar Khayyám? And it is the transmutation of these into our virile English tongue by the subtle alchemy of Edward Fitz-Gerald that has secured him an everlasting name.'

Fitz-Gerald's fame rests upon his Persian translations, and I need not enter into details respecting those which he made from the Greek. As he said they were intended to interest persons who knew not the original; he thought they might be more attracted by his curious version in which textual difficulties were disposed of in a summary manner, than they would be by translations of greater ability. But by his droll mode of publication this class of readers was not likely to see the pamphlets which he had provided for their edification. His translation from Sophocles was partly done, and then dropped for several years; he only completed it when strongly urged to do so by Professor Norton. In this case he united two Tragedies in one Drama, which, he said, was neither a paraphrase nor a translation of Sophocles, but chiefly taken from him.

His version of the 'Agamemnon' was equally daring. He printed a few copies to give away, but they had neither name of author, title-page, nor imprint, and were issued in a hideous cover of grocers' azure.[1] From scholars in America there came a demand for what he called 'this version or perversion of Æschylus,' and Mr Quaritch asked to be allowed to reprint it on his own account. The request was granted, 'but,' said Fitz-Gerald, 'Quaritch will print it so pretentiously that it looks as if one thought it very precious. For, whatever the merits of it may be, it can't come near all this fine paper, margin, etc.' So modesty had its way to the last.

[1] *Fortnightly Review*, July 1889.

Edward Fitz-Gerald

HIS LIBRARY AND HIS CRITICISMS.

Fitz-Gerald's distaste for society caused him to keep within the walls of his own home, and the companionship of books became one of the greatest elements in his happiness. Sitting in the room in which some of his favourite volumes were stored, he would take down a volume for the fifth or sixth time, and was as well pleased as if he were having a hearty shake of the hand from a dear old friend. He had as much affection for his books as he had for a dog or any living animal. He divided them, as he divided men, into sheep and goats, and those which he selected were to him not dead things; they spoke to him of men and times of the past, which had left their impression to enrich the present. His favour-

… ites were those in which the writers were transparent—men and women who exhibited themselves in the printed page, and with whom he could hold sweet communion, as if they were bodily present in his room. His ability as a linguist gave an extra zest to his reading, as it enabled him to read the works of the giants of literature—French, Spanish, German, Italian, and Persian, in the language in which they were penned. Ascetic as he was in many respects, books full of passion and tenderness were to him pearls of great price. Even a cursory perusal of his letters will show how extensive was his reading, how discriminating was his criticism, and a library which contained side by side John Henry Newman's *Parochial Sermons*, *The Quatrains of Omar Khayyám*, Montaigne's *Essays*, and John Wesley's *Journal*, shows his catholicity as well as eclectic taste.

His collection of books was not so large as one might expect a gentleman of wealth

Edward Fitz-Gerald

and culture to get together, but it embraced works in a variety of languages, and on a diversity of subjects. Science was apparently neglected, whilst history was only sparingly recognized. He was at no pains to secure the complete works of any author, but he selected for his library what he deemed the best productions of his favourites, and his judgment was not often at fault. Wordsworth's own library was said to have been one of the most wretched that ever went by that name—a mere litter of tattered odd volumes on a few shelves. The smallness of Carlyle's library, perhaps the smallest, excepting mere books of reference, that ever belonged to a great man of letters, was notorious. Fitz-Gerald's was very different from these, as it extended to considerably more than a thousand volumes. With his books he was most intimately acquainted; he could easily and lovingly discourse on their contents, and with the peculiarities of their authors he was no less familiar.

The Life of

He had no mania for rare books; at any rate he did not purchase them because they were rare. Neither did he feel prompted to lay out his money on first editions. He had first editions of Tennyson and Thackeray, but they were presentation copies from his two dear old friends. He judged a book by its contents, no factitious or conventional value—such as large paper, tall or uncut copies, which would be proudly offered by a bookseller, had any influence on his judgment. Folio or quarto volumes he disliked (though he had some of each) as they were not handy to use. He liked a book that he could carry to the fire and hold readily in his hand. In 1834 he bought a second and also a third folio of Shakespeare, and they delighted him much, but later in life, the Cambridge edition being octavo was his favourite book for use, whenever he wanted to refer to the 'sweet swan of Avon!'

He did not appreciate ornamental binding, and very few volumes on his shelves

Edward Fitz-Gerald

were decorated by special tooling. Some were bound in vellum, some in Russia, but these were works which were printed and bound in Paris, Madrid, or Amsterdam. Some two or three hundred volumes were half calf, green with red label. These were bound by a Woodbridge bookbinder, and Fitz-Gerald had them done in this style, because many of them were placed in the room which he used most, and the colour suited his failing eyesight. Judging from the appearance of his books as a whole, he probably never had a volume bound by Zhaensdorf or Riviere, or any such artistic bookbinder in his life. A few volumes appeared in half morocco, but most of them were dingy in look, in cloth bindings as issued by the publishers, or if old were calf or half calf as purchased. His neighbour and friend Captain Brooke of Ufford, gloried in having his books bound in the best and most artistic style. Not so Fitz-Gerald. Only three works of his were adorned, even with gilt edges. Tusser's *Five Hundred Points of Good Husbandry* was clothed in half red morocco, gilt, with top edge gilt, and Major Moor's *Suffolk Words and Phrases* was bound in morocco, extra gilt, but these came from his father's library.

One small book attracted attention, and hereby hangs a tale. This special volume, bound in dark green morocco extra, was *Songs of Innocence* by William Blake, the mystic poet, who was his own illustrator. Fitz-Gerald bought this when he was only twenty-two years of age, and writing to his friend W. B. Donne soon afterwards he says, ' I have lately bought a little pamphlet, which is very difficult to get, called the *Songs of Innocence*, written and adorned with three coloured drawings by W. Blake, who it was said was quite mad, but his madness was really the elements of genius ill sorted; when I see you I will show you this book.' Fitz-Gerald does not say what this small pamphlet cost him, probably only a

Edward Fitz-Gerald

few shillings, but at the sale of his books at Sotheby & Wilkinson's, this dainty little volume realised £34!

Many other volumes from his library sold well at Sotheby's. Thackeray's books fetched high prices. *The Second Funeral of Napoleon* and the *Chronicles of the Drum*, illustrated but unbound, were knocked down at £6, 10s. But the gem of Thackeray's books in the sale was his *Illustrations to Undine*. It had no title, but one was supplied in bistre with ornamental design in the centre, and sixteen water colour drawings were inserted, all designed and executed by Thackeray's own hand. This volume bound in dark green morocco brought £17. There was a note on the fly-leaf by Fitz-Gerald thus:—'The drawings in this volume were made by W. M. Thackeray, as we sat talking together, two mornings in the spring of 1835 or 1836 at the house of his stepfather, Carmichael Smith, in Albion Street, Hyde Park, London.'

The Life of

Thackeray, like Hogarth, could always make his pictures tell his story, and looking at the wit and humour displayed in many of his sketches, good judges have felt that had he applied himself to this department of Art, he would have been a second Hogarth. He used to throw about his pen and ink drawings as if they were worth nothing. FitzGerald had an album full of them. They were executed by the artist during the twenty years 1829 to 1849.

'Little Grange,' the house in which he last lived, was not particularly small, but as his nieces every year occupied the best rooms, he was restricted as to places for shelving, and his books were necessarily scattered about. The study, as the room was called, in which he more commonly than not lived and slept, was partitioned off so as to make two rooms, one for sleeping, the other for meals and reading and writing; each was about fifteen feet by seventeen. The living room which had, in French style,

Edward Fitz-Gerald

large folding glazed doors opening into the garden, had bookshelves on two sides, and there was more shelving in the bedroom. The front entrance by the porch was also shelved.

Other volumes were placed in handsome cases in the dining and drawing rooms. Many volumes were piled under the staircase; in one of his letters he speaks of books which he wished to consult being inconveniently stowed away in a dark closet. One of his eccentric habits was to pull leaves out of books. Sometimes this iconoclasm extended to an entire section. These were pages which he deemed mere padding, and he thought the book would be improved by their removal. But a still more extraordinary habit in connection with his books was revealed after his death. He was in the habit of withdrawing from the bank some sixty or seventy pounds at a time for general expenses. His executors having obtained the keys from Merton Rectory, where Mr.

Fitz-Gerald died, unlocked his desk, and finding no cash, made inquiry of the housekeeper. 'Mr. Fitz-Gerald,' she replied, 'generally drew his money in bank notes, and he kept them for security between the leaves of several books on that shelf,' pointing to one nearest the head of the bed. The idea of hunting for five-pound notes, among the leaves of an indiscriminate lot of volumes on a certain shelf, made the executors stare. But search was instantly made, and before it was given up, some thirty or forty pounds in notes were rescued from the leaves of these old volumes. If any purchaser at the sale found a note among the books he bought, the fact was not made known either to the executors or to the auctioneer.

It has been said that the book lover is known by his book-plate, the outward sign of the true lover of literature. Fitz-Gerald, as we have said, had no strong feeling for rare or curious books, and would never have

Edward Fitz-Gerald

adorned his notepaper with a gold or silver monogram, but he considered it 'correct' to have a book-plate, affixed within the covers of each of his volumes, to act as a label and herald of his ownership. Fitz-Gerald's book-plate is one of those modern examples that has an interest both artistic and personal. The talents of Sir William Boxall, Sir John Millais, Walter Crane, Stacy Marks, Kate Greenaway, and others, had been called into requisition by various lovers of literature to design book-plates for them, and it was a happy thought of Fitz-Gerald's to ask his friend Thackeray to sketch one for him. This he did, and afterwards, in his good-natured way, made the drawing on the wood block for the engraver. It was done one morning in 1842, when these staunch friends were together in London. It is small in size and belongs to the class of heraldic allegoric. The subject is an angel holding a shield at her breast, with armorial bearings, the name E. Fitz-Gerald being

The Life of

below. It is said that in the angel Thackeray portrayed Mrs Brookfield. This book-plate is scarce, and among collectors invariably fetches a good price. Mrs Brookfield was the wife of the Rev. William Henry Brookfield, a dear friend of Tennyson and Thackeray's, of whom Dr. Thompson, the Master of Trinity College said, 'he was far the most amusing man I ever met.'

Taking a general glance at his library, we see a selection of works which did justice alike to his taste and judgment; at the same time it presents to our view those literary companions of his solitary life, from which he picked his bosom friends. Taking them in sections they were as follows :—

DRAMATIC.

Shakespeare's Dramatic Works (several editions); Sir John Vambrugh's Plays; Gray's 'Beggars' Opera'; George Lillo's

Edward Fitz-Gerald

Dramatic Works; Kemble's 'Notes on Shakespeare'; Lamb's 'Specimens of Early English Dramatic Poets'; Hazlitt's 'View of the English Stage'; Fitz-Gerald's 'Life of David Garrick'; Boaden's 'Memoir of John Philip Kemble'; Macready's 'Reminiscences'; Fanny Kemble's 'Records of a Girlhood'; Marlowe's Works; Molière's Works, in French and English; Lumley's 'Reminiscences of the Opera'; Calderon's D'Pedro Comedies; Sophocles; Euripides; and Aristophanes.

Dictionaries, &c.

Johnson's Persian, Arabic, and English Dictionary; Jamieson's 'Dictionary of the Scotch Language'; Arabic, Anglo-Saxon, Danish, and Norse Grammars; Halliwell's 'Dictionary of Provincial Words'; Spanish and Italian Dictionaries; Greek Lexicon; Richardson's 'Persian, Arabic, and English Vocabulary.'

The Life of

Fine Arts.

Pilkington's 'Dictionary of Painters'; Leslie's 'Life of Constable'; Fulcher's 'Life of Gainsborough'; 'Life of Sir David Wilkie'; Krugler's 'Handbook of Painting'; German, Flemish, and Dutch Schools; Bewick's 'Land and Water Birds'; 'Our People,' Sketched by Charles Keene (from the Collection of Mr. Punch); Hogarth's Works; 'Our Old Inns,' by Edwin Edwards.

Essays and General Literature.

Madame De Sevigne's 'Letters' (several editions); Montaigne's 'Essais,' also the first English Translation of Montaigne's 'Essays'; Hazlitt's 'Table Talk'; Coleridge's 'Table Talk'; 'Essays of Elia'; Ray's 'Collection of English Proverbs'; Moor's 'Suffolk Words and Phrases'; Thomas Moore's Memoirs and Journal; Emerson's 'Essays'; 'Correspondence of Carlyle and Emerson'; Goethe's 'Conversations

Edward Fitz-Gerald

with Eckermann'; 'Correspondence between Schiller and Goethe'; Pepys' 'Diary and Correspondence'; Bacon's Works; Pascal's Letters; Milton's Prose Works; Plato's 'Republic'; Sale's 'Koran'; Sydney Smith's Works; Crabbe Robinson's 'Diary'; Macaulay's Letters and Miscellaneous Writings; Trench on the Study of Words; Life and Letters of Keats; 'Selections from the Letters of Southey'; De Quincey's Works; Professor Wilson's Works; Lockhart's 'Life of Scott'; John Wesley's 'Journal'; White's 'Selbourne.'

MUSIC AND MUSICIANS.

Holme's 'Life and Correspondence of Mozart'; Beethoven's 'Letters'; Mendelssohn's 'Letters'; 'Letters of Distinguished Musicians'; Spohr's 'Autobiography'; Rossini's Memoirs; Chorley's 'Modern German Music'; Chorley's 'Thirty Years' Musical Recollections'; Gretory, 'Memoires Sur la Musique'; Fetis (M), 'La Musique.'

The Life of

Poets and Poetry.

Tennyson's Works; Tennyson Turner's 'Sonnets and Lyrics'; Crabbe's 'Poetical Works'; Rogers' 'Poems'; Wordsworth's Works; Keat's Poetical Works; Milton's Poetical Works; 'Don Juan'; Chaucer's 'Canterbury Tales'; Hood's Works; Homer's 'Iliad' and 'Odyssey'; Dante; Virgil; 'Omár Kháyyám's Quatrains,' translated into English verse by Whinfield; also Paris edition by J. B. Nicolas; 'Petrarque' (Fr.); Aeuyres Hafiz (Dewan) Works in Persian.

Fiction.

Sir Walter Scott's Works; the principal works of Dickens, Thackeray, and Hawthorne; 'Clarissa Harlowe' (two editions); 'Arabian Nights'; 'Pilgrim's Progress'; 'Joseph Andrews'; 'Don Quixote' (four editions); 'Gil Blas'; Boccaccio's 'Decameron.'

Edward Fitz-Gerald

When Fitz-Gerald was in his prime, and settled at Woodbridge, he made the acquaintance of an old bookseller residing in Ipswich, whose society for some years he very much enjoyed, and on whom he bestowed some of his patronage. This was Mr. James Read, who lived at the corner of the thoroughfare, on the east side of the present post office buildings. His 'Old Booke Shoppe' became famous to lovers of literature, through the treasures which they found therein. Mr. Read himself, however, was as much renowned as his books. The very appearance of the man, as he stood behind his counter, at once proclaimed him a kindred spirit of Fitz-Gerald's, and unmistakably a man of mark. There he was, a broad-shouldered man of medium height, large features, high cheek bones, with a good colour in his face, clean shaven, with a stand up collar upheld by a satin stock, which had seen its best days. His head was invariably covered by a tall hat, set well back on his head, and noted for its antique appearance. He wore a swallow-tail coat, which one could see was of black cloth, but, although well brushed, its cut and dingy look gave the visitor the impression that it might have been in use when its owner commenced business. A black apron completed his attire. I have said that Mr. Read was to the lover of old books as attractive as his stock. To some he was more so. Extensive reading and extraordinary memory had made him a walking encyclopædia. Many a student has had good reason to be grateful to him for advice as to where he could find materials that would elucidate the subject he was investigating. A nonconformist himself, he had made the rise of dissenters in England a special study, and in the history of puritanism his knowledge was unrivalled. The true bookworm always enjoyed half an hour's chat with him, densely surrounded as he was with curiosities of literature, in a shop that offered the best

Edward Fitz-Gerald

possible proof that its occupier had a horror of whitewash. Such book lovers as William Powell Hunt, Francis Capper Brooke, William Stevenson Fitch, Edward Acton, and Professor Cowell were sure to be met with every now and then in his shop. Fitz-Gerald would lounge in and ramble round the place, taking down various volumes as he walked along, pointing out their beauties or defects in a manner which showed extensive knowledge. He was particularly fond of John Wesley's Journal, and frequently bought copies of Mr. Read to give away. This was one of the books which he considered he could greatly improve by scissors, but although this project was often talked of, it was never carried out. Mr. Read could not be considered a shrewd tradesman. He scarcely conducted his business in the trading spirit. You could buy what you wished or leave it alone. He used to lament that book buyers were so few, not from a sense of personal loss as regards profit, but from a public point of view. A non-reading public was a stupid public, would be his contention. At the same time, his shop was more for students than for the casual purchaser. If you appeared to be a clergyman, Mr. Read would probably relieve his mind upon the conventional style of Christianity, which suited the professional exponent and the majority of mankind, but for which he had nothing short of contempt. Many a clergyman must have had an uncomfortable quarter of an hour in that old dingy shop. At the same time Mr. Read's candour was refreshing, and he attacked systems rather than men.

One Sunday morning Mr. Read received a letter from Fitz-Gerald asking his company at dinner on the following day at 'Little Grange.' A conveyance was hired, and Mr. Read's partner drove him to Woodbridge. Having stabled the horse at the 'Royal Oak,' he walked on to 'Little Grange' and rang the bell. The housekeeper, Mrs.

Edward Fitz-Gerald

How, speedily made her appearance. 'I've called to see Mr. Fitz-Gerald,' says Mr. Read. 'You can't see him to-day, sir,' responded the housekeeper. 'But I've come from Ipswich by his invitation.' 'Can't help it, sir, you will not see him to-day,' was the prompt reply. Mr. Read was staggered. He fumbled in his breast pocket, and brought out Fitz-Gerald's letter to see if he made a mistake as to the time. No; there it was plain enough; he had called exactly at the time mentioned; but as the housekeeper's tone showed that she did not mean to admit him to the house, he trudged back to the 'Royal Oak,' had lunch, and chewed the cud of disappointment as he was driven home, not forgetting that on a previous visit Fitz-Gerald had provided a good dinner, with a bottle of Scotch ale, whilst the host, instead of sitting down to the entertainment, ambled about the room like a caged lion, munching a big apple, discussing meanwhile literary topics of interest to both. The day after the drive to Woodbridge, Mr. Read received a letter from Fitz-Gerald stating, 'I saw you yesterday when you called, but I was not fit for company, and felt I could not be bothered.' Nothing more inconsiderate can be found among the whimsicalities of George Borrow.

In one of his letters, Fitz-Gerald speaks of Captain Brooke of Ufford, as being 'our one man of books down here.' In making this remark he doubtless thought as much of Mr Brooke's scholarship and accurate knowledge of books as of the magnificent library, upwards of twenty thousand volumes, which that gentleman had with zeal and money collected, and with which Fitz-Gerald often enjoyed himself to his heart's content. This remarkable collection ranked among the finest private collections in England. A gentleman who knew it and its owner well says, 'Captain Brooke's acquirements as a bibliographer were surprising to those who were not acquainted with the large amount

Edward Fitz-Gerald

of time and money that he had devoted to the study of that science. If fortune had not made him a country gentleman, he would have been eminent amongst booksellers. He spared neither trouble nor expense in making his selections. On one occasion he travelled all the way to Rome to attend a sale of books. His was a familiar face at most of the great sales in this country. It was his invariable practice to obtain not only the best books, but the best copies. In one respect his collection was unique, some of the more valuable works being author's copies, annotated for use in future editions.'

Captain Brooke was something more than a mere book buyer. He was well acquainted with the contents of the best works in several languages, and having an excellent memory, could supply information upon most topics with the utmost ease, while he was seldom at a loss in finding the necessary authorities upon all kinds of odd or abstruse subjects. Nothing gave him greater pleasure than to place his library at the disposal of readers and students. He was often heard to say that the one thing he most regretted was that more literary men did not avail themselves of the opportunity he offered, and the only condition he imposed was that other people should treat his books with something of the care which he himself manifested — that they should be gently handled, and returned to their proper places on the shelves. From all this it may readily be supposed that Fitz-Gerald felt himself thoroughly at home both with the library and its owner.

Having in previous pages glanced at the contents of Fitz-Gerald's library, I would now draw attention to those criticisms on literature and art which are to be found in the published volumes of his *Letters*.

These criticisms are of striking significance, not simply because he wrote in a way not easily forgotten, but because the reader

Edward Fitz-Gerald

finds himself in close alliance with a good scholar, free and unconstrained, and nobly generous. They exhibit his fine and acute perception; are brisk, fresh, and appropriate. It will be admitted that, as a conscientious man, Fitz-Gerald pronounced judgment on men and things in a kindly spirit, and with the authority of intellectual power and keen discrimination. Any reader who does not endorse his verdicts will generally admire the independence which, if not a guarantee of perfection, is a bond of fidelity as between writer and reader. You read a man's work for his convictions, and there is no difficulty in getting at Fitz-Gerald's.

Fitz-Gerald had old-fashioned tastes, and in poetry a great love for the ancients. His poetical instincts deepened his love for the Greek poets, but of them he was not a wide reader. Greek poetry to him chiefly meant Homer, Æschylus, and Sophocles.

His love for old English poetry was so great that he failed to do justice to some

The Life of

modern poets. Of Ebenezer Elliot's poems he had an exalted opinion. Longfellow he loved, but Shelley was too unsubstantial. Browning, with all his power and richness, failed to win his approbation. Swinburne he described as a fiery, unquiet spirit. Of Keats he was an ardent admirer. When writing to Frederick Tennyson, he advised him to beg, borrow, steal, or buy Keats' *Letters and Poems*. With the Suffolk poet, Crabbe, he was, to use a Suffolk phrase, wrapped up; him he was always quoting or readjusting. Tennyson was one of his dearest friends, but this did not prevent Fitz-Gerald from applying trenchant criticism to some of his works. The earlier poems delighted him, but of *In Memoriam* he said, 'It is full of the finest things, but it is monotonous.' *The Northern Farmer* and some of the *Idylls* struck his fancy, as they have the fancy of so many others. He granted that, as a man of genius, Tennyson might 'still surprise us by poems that will

Edward Fitz-Gerald

atone for what seem to me latter day failures.' Fitz-Gerald did not live to read *Crossing the Bar*, otherwise he would have found that the English people took to it almost as a divine conception.

In the world of Fiction he revelled in Sir Walter Scott's works. When he engaged a reader he set him night after night to read the Waverley novels. His sense of appreciation may be seen in this—'I feel in parting with each volume as parting with an old friend whom I may never see again.' Of Dickens he wrote — 'I for one worship Dickens in spite of Carlyle and the critics, and wish to see his Gad's Hill, as I wished to see Shakespeare's Stratford and Scott's Abbotsford.' In his latter years Thackeray's novels were to him terrible; he looked at them on the shelf, but seemed reluctant to touch them. Fitz-Gerald acknowledged that his books were wonderful, but they were not delightful, and delight 'one thirsts for as one gets old and dry.' He was very pleased with *Barchester Towers*, which, though not perfect, was perfect enough to make him feel that he knew the people, even if caricatured or carelessly drawn. Ultimately Trollope had no more ardent admirer. Twenty years before his decease he said, 'I am now reading *Clarissa Harlowe* for the fifth time.' He preferred the sentimentalism of Richardson to the realism of Fielding. Miss Austen's novels remained without a rival in Macaulay's affections, but by them Fitz-Gerald was not smitten. 'I think Miss Austen quite capable, in a circle I have found quite unendurable to walk in.' He could not take to George Eliot's novels, and though recognising Hawthorne as the most marked man of genius America had produced in the way of imagination, yet he never found any appetite for his books.

These brief notes will convey a faint idea of Fitz-Gerald's criticisms. Fragments they are, but they will, I trust, induce my readers to turn at once to Fitz-Gerald's *Letters to*

Edward Fitz-Gerald

Fanny Kemble, and to the two-volume edition of Fitz-Gerald's *Letters*, published in the Eversley Series, where they will find copious and keen criticisms on literature, music, and art. In fact these *Letters* are indispensable to those who desire to understand the critical power of the man.

The Life of

CARLYLE'S VISIT TO FITZ-GERALD AT WOODBRIDGE.

At the death of his father, in 1852, Edward Fitz-Gerald's housekeeping at the Bungalow came to an end. The Boulge Hall estate descended to Mr. John Purcell Fitz-Gerald, the eldest son, with whom Edward was not on the most cordial terms. They were, he said, good friends, but theological differences kept them apart. At any rate, when his brother died, he acknowledged that he had not been inside his park gates (only three miles from Woodbridge) for a dozen years. Nor did he enter them on the occasion of the funeral. With another brother, Peter, who had embraced the Roman Catholic faith, he was on the most affectionate terms, but the eldest brother was an evangelical churchman of a very low type; in him, too, were concentrated

Edward Fitz-Gerald

all the eccentricities of the Fitz-Gerald family, but theology was doubtless the stumbling-block between the brothers in the path of intimacy.

Fitz-Gerald's furniture, books, and pictures were stowed away at a farm house, Farlingay Hall, not far from the Bungalow. He was on the best of terms with the farmer and his wife, and not being anxious to take another house, he sometimes stayed with them a month at a time; with his friend Parson Crabbe he was off and on for two months, then he would float about for a year or two and visit distant friends. He would run down to the Isle of Wight, or to Shropshire to see Allen, or to Bath to see one of his sisters, in whose company he had scarcely been for six years. When he arrived at Bath, he wrote to Frederick Tennyson, 'You see to what fashionable places I am reduced in my old age.'

He continued roving about, but the most important of his visits was that to his old friend Archdeacon Allen at Prees Vicarage, near Shrewsbury. He had long talked of going there, but delays with him were proverbial, and almost in envy he remarked one day that 'young Churchyard makes less fuss of his prospective trip to America than I do of a journey to Shropshire. He had so low an estimate of the value of his company, that he did not hesitate to let his friends 'wait a long time before he went to occupy their easy chairs.' But once in Allen's vicarage home he enjoyed himself thoroughly; in fact, it seemed that whilst in the company of his old friend, he was inspired with all the freshness and fun of his college days. They had long country walks daily, and evenings were devoted to the recall of reminiscences of old college days and college friends. With the children Fitz-Gerald was a great favourite; he adapted a French play for their performance, and amused them by extemporising music as fast as an ordinary man would

Edward Fitz-Gerald

write a letter. Sometimes a six-year-old little girl accompanied them in their walks, and when they came to a style, Fitz-Gerald lifted her over with the cheery words, 'Now, little Ticket!' On one Sunday afternoon he accompanied his friend to a neighbouring village, where, the incumbent having just lost his wife, the Archdeacon had kindly undertaken the duty. On their return, Mrs Allen inquired how they found the widower. 'Rather lachrymose,' replied Fitz-Gerald, in his humorous way. The choir had 'struck' just before his visit, and a harmonium was inaugurated the first Sunday of his stay. Fitz-Gerald undertook to preside, and he told the Archdeacon's eldest son that he was to make it known that the congregation that morning would have the opportunity of listening to the performance of a distinguished foreigner, Signor Geraldino.

In the early part of his London life, Fitz-Gerald was frequently with Thackeray. In taste and disposition they had so much in common that they became quite companions, but even then Fitz-Gerald was so shy that he would not attend the parties which Thackeray had at his mother's house. The great novelist became the object of aristocratic patronage during the publication of *Vanity Fair*, and whilst this conviviality and money-making was going on, Fitz-Gerald saw less and less of his old friend, and thought himself neglected. His fears as to Thackeray's forgetfulness were, however, thrown to the winds when Fitz-Gerald saw it announced that he was going to lecture in America. Writing to W. B. Donne, he says: 'Dear old Thackeray is going to America; I must fire him a letter of farewell.' Thackeray was much touched by this letter. Before leaving England, he sent a reply in which, in the most tender manner, he took leave of his friend. It began,

'My Dearest Old Friend,—I must not go away without shaking your hand, and saying farewell and God bless you.'

Edward Fitz-Gerald

And he said further, if anything happened to him, he would like his daughters to remember that Fitz-Gerald was not only the oldest, but the best friend their father ever had. The last sentence of the letter ran thus:—

'I care for you, as you know, and always like to think that I am fondly and affectionately yours.—W. M. T.'

Fitz-Gerald's response to this letter was characteristic. After mentioning that he had by will provided that the sum of £500 after his decease should be paid to Thackeray's eldest daughter, he says, 'You owe me no thanks for giving what I can no longer use. It will be some satisfaction to me to know that your generous friendship bore some sort of fruit, if not to yourself, to those you are naturally anxious about.'

It is a matter of observation that friendship often springs up between the most unlikely persons, and maintains its vitality under widely different circumstances, and with great contrasts of character. This was especially the case with Fitz-Gerald and Carlyle. Before their personal acquaintance began, Fitz-Gerald could not tolerate Carlyle's style of writing, but after a few years' intercourse, he declared that he did not find it tiresome, any more than he did his talk to listen to, which always delighted him. He said his writing was only the talk of a great genius put on paper for general perusal; that so far from being wearisome to read, as he advanced in years, he thought it had become better. They were as one in their strong desire for simplicity of life, and in their hatred of every species of cant. Carlyle kept aloof from the bitterness and turmoil of English party politics, and Fitz-Gerald, when writing to his friend Frederick Tennyson, said, 'Don't write politics, I agree with you beforehand.'

As years passed on this friendship was so strongly cemented that, in 1855, Fitz-Gerald invited Carlyle to spend his Summer holiday with him at Woodbridge, and this

Edward Fitz-Gerald

invitation the Chelsea sage accepted. When he solicited Carlyle to visit him, he had not a house himself to live in. For two or three years he had been roving about the country, his furniture being, as I have mentioned, packed away at a farm house. This farm house, known as Farlingay Hall, was one of the large old-fashioned 'Halls' which, as Manor houses, formerly abounded in Suffolk, and as there was plenty of accommodation, Fitz-Gerald induced the farmer and his wife to let Carlyle and himself have apartments for a short time in their pretty rural home. He had already inquired of Mrs Carlyle what it was desirable to procure for her husband in the way of food, stating that he knew his wants were in small compass, and that it was easy to get what he liked if she would only say. The result was a stay of more than a week, to Carlyle's great enjoyment.

This visit began on August 8th, 1855. Fitz-Gerald had given full instructions for

The Life of

the journey, and Carlyle decided to leave Shoreditch Station at 11 a.m., being due at Ipswich about 2. There E. F.-G. met him, and, after looking about the old town, at Carlyle's desire they drove direct to Farlingay Hall. Carlyle brought books with him, gave all parties a good hint that he wished sometimes to be left alone, as he was used to several hours of solitude every day, and did not grow *weary* of it, though he was willing to be driven to any place Fitz-Gerald recommended. The two friends journeyed together to have a look at Aldeburgh, at the ruined city of Dunwich, and at the famous castle of Framlingham.

The day after his arrival, Fitz-Gerald marched his visitor off to Bredfield Rectory to be introduced to the Rev. George Crabbe, and thither they afterwards went two or three days in succession. Carlyle was delighted with the frank and hearty manner of the parson, and was pleased to have a talk with his eldest daughter, a clever

Edward Fitz-Gerald

woman, a great reader who could recollect what she read, though she always gave her opinion very modestly. It was harvest time, and in the evenings the three friends sat out on the lawn, smoking and discussing various themes to their hearts' content. Carlyle's wonderful range of conversation surprised all who listened to him. The farmer at Farlingay Hall was astonished to find that he was as conversant with soils and crops as if he had been all his life tilling the land. Whilst sitting on the lawn, under the shadow of a fine tree, Carlyle poured forth his invectives on the men and manners of the day, whenever he removed his pipe from his lips. He was vociferous in his denunciations of shams and windbags, and once declared that Burns ought to have been king of England, and George III. the exciseman. Some of his smart sayings left their impression, as, 'Piety does not mean that a man should make a sour face about things, and refuse to enjoy in moderation what his Maker has given.' On his return home he wrote to Mr. Crabbe, thanking him for the way in which he had contributed to his enjoyment during his stay at Woodbridge, and expressed the pleasure he had in meeting his daughter.

Carlyle was so delighted by his visit that he even proposed to renew it, and in writing to Fitz-Gerald suggested that when he got his little Suffolk cottage there must be a chamber in the wall for him. If, in addition, there was a pony that he could ride, and a cow that gave good milk, they could have a pretty rustication now and then. This idea did not last long with him. He found he could not sleep so well on his return home, the change was too great. The stillness which surrounded him at Farlingay Hall was unattainable at Chelsea, and as he lost a second sleep every night he gave up all thoughts of again rusticating in the quietude of a Suffolk village. At the same time he was confident of being benefited by his

Edward Fitz-Gerald

visit, ' and by all the kindness of my beneficent brother mortals to me there.' The latter years of his life he passed in a very feeble condition, and Fitz-Gerald seldom called, as he found that conversation exhausted him, but he always had him in memory. The strength of his feeling towards his friend may be judged by the fact that not long before his death, being in London, he was almost tempted to jump into a cab, just knock at Carlyle's door, ask after him, give his card and run away.

From Froude's biography the public learnt of Carlyle's love for his own family, his generosity to them, and his struggles to help to maintain his father and mother out of very slender earnings. All this intensified Fitz-Gerald's regard for him. He frequently expressed his regret that he did not know whilst Carlyle was alive what the book told him, that he might have *loved* as well as admired him during their friendly intercourse — this being a phase of Carlyle's

The Life of

character which he **had** not taken into account before. This loving memory for his friend remained with Fitz-Gerald to the last.

Carlyle, on the other hand, had an equally strong esteem for Fitz-Gerald. His letters show how ardently he desired to see or hear from him, often regretting that communications came so seldom, and the inquiry in person not at all. 'Are you never to see London and us again? After the beginning of next week I am at Chelsea, and there is a fire in the evening now to welcome you there; show your face in some way or other. I beg to be kept in remembrance as probably your oldest friend.'

The following letters from Carlyle to Fitz-Gerald will help to show the strength of their attachment.

'Chelsea, December 7th, 1868.

'DEAR FITZ-GERALD,—Thanks for inquiring after me again. I am in my usual

Edward Fitz-Gerald

weak state of bodily health, not much worse I imagine, and not even expecting to be better. I study to be solitary, in general; to be silent, as the state that suits me best; my thoughts then are infinitely sad indeed, but capable too of being solemn, mournfully beautiful, useful; and as for "happiness," I have that of employment more or less befitting the years I have arrived at, and the long journey that cannot now be far off.

'Your letter has really entertained me; I could willingly accept twelve of that kind in the year—twelve, I say, or even fifty-two, if they could be content with an answer of *silent* thanks and friendly thoughts and remembrances! But within the last three or four years my right hand has become captious, taken to shaking as you see, and all writing is a thing I require *compulsion* and close necessity to drive me into! Why not call here when you come to town? I again assure you it would give me pleasure, and be a welcome and wholesome solace to me. With many true wishes and regards, I am always, Dear F., sincerely yours,

'T. CARLYLE.'

'*Chelsea, 31st October* 1869.

'DEAR FITZ-GERALD,—I have not much to say in reply to your kind letter of inquiry, except that *it* is very welcome to me, and my regret only is that the like comes so seldom, and the inquiry in person never at all! The sight of you again would no doubt bring mournful memories, but it would surely do me good withal.

'For the last year I have been extremely bothered with *want of sleep;* a miserable kind of suffering—coming always at intervals, though too frequently, and much deranging my poor proceedings for the time it lasts. Within the last few weeks, it has again nearly withdrawn, and I am again flattering myself that it will not return, but leave me at my old poor level,

Edward Fitz-Gerald

which you know was never very high! A brother of mine (M.D. by profession) asserts, plausibly rather, that good part of the mischief has arisen from the employment I was at :—sorting, etc., etc., of old papers pertaining to the dead and vanished; which naturally kept me in an altogether sombre state of mind, and that now this or the *tenderest* part of this being mainly done, rest will follow. We shall see, we shall see!

'I had a most still life here; my thoughts turned mostly far elsewhither, as is now fit and suitable. They are printing a "Library Edition," as they call it, of my poor books; five or six proof-sheets came to-day, which I think myself bound to read. This is pretty much my one *prescribed* employment, but I have enough of *others* very much more interesting to me. With one or two (I really think hardly four in all) I have now and then some pleasant conversation, the other mostly. I am better without. In short, I am becoming a land hermit as much as you are a sea one.

'Browning's book I read, *insisted* on reading: it is full of talent, of energy, and effort, but totally without backbone or vein of common-sense. I think, among the absurdest books ever written by a gifted man. Do you know the late Arthur Clough and his Writings and Biography, edited by his widow (Macmillan & Co.)? Let me recommend that to you: I knew Clough, and loved him well.

'Adieu, dear F., you see what my *right hand* is gone to, though my heart is still alive as ever.—Yours truly,

'T. CARLYLE.'

'*Chelsea, 7th December* 186 .

'DEAR FITZ-GERALD,—What a time since we have seen you! And still it is no visit, it is only the arrival of half-yearly note—better than quite nothing.

'We did not quit town at all this year:

Edward Fitz-Gerald

the wife ran to Ramsgate with a lady friend, to taste the sea air—was delighted with the sea air, but like to be driven mad by the brass bands, bagpipes, Ethiopians, hawkers, and perpetual ragings of foul . . . (not to mention the nasty fat Jews and fat-bellied Cockneys), and came home in a week. I sit here under an awning, and the shadow of the back wall, obstinately bungling along at this unblessed task of mine—and might as well have flung it aside, for my rate of "progress" was frightful. We went in September for about ten days into Windsor Forest; some goodish galloping I had in the noble Park there (though under lumbago, etc.), and that was all the rustication vouchsafed to us this year.

'I am now really pretty well in health considering the years I count and the drudgery I have to stick to—if I could get done with the latter, I should really be tolerably off. But alas, the goal is still far away, and sad muddy pilgrimage, and months more than I like to reckon, are loaded with chagrin, disgust, and almost despair, before the deliverance can come. In the mean time I continue *buried*; see nobody (go to see absolutely nobody), toil and struggle all hours of the day, with whatever strength is left me, towards this as the one good still possible for me. With a kind of indignation for most part (for myself among other people), which, as it is all *silent*, does the less ill. In truth, "this ten years among the Prussian pots" has made me very grimy, and humiliated me to the very marrow of the bone. I was computing lately, in one of my rides, that I must have ridden (upon my excellent horse Fritz, who is now waxing old as doth a garment) something like 20,000 miles,—nineteen-twentieths of it or more in solitude, since I began this hateful adventure!

'My poor wife is but weakly, has had a tedious cold, etc., but is now getting better. Are you never to see London again, and us

Edward Fitz-Gerald

again? You have still that stone to set up on Naseby Moor, remember! It was indeed a miserable oversight not to go on to Edinburgh when so near it. Courage! I will drag you there some day myself. Adieu, dear F.—Yours ever,

'T. CARLYLE.'

Fitz-Gerald, eccentric himself, was occasionally visited by other eccentrics. One of these was a man who for a time became famous, and to-day has his worshippers. This was George Borrow—author of 'The Bible in Spain.' His tall, erect, and somewhat mysterious figure made its appearance unexpectedly at Fitz-Gerald's apartments, and as he was known to be master of many languages, and was fully conversant with Spanish, the way seemed clear for mutual attachment. Fitz-Gerald did not, however, admire Borrow's translations, and said that as years rolled on his taste became stranger than ever. He first met him at his friend's

The Life of

W. B. Donne's, at Bury St. Edmunds, when his masterful way and his blunt manner at once impressed him, whilst his shaggy eyebrows, by shading his keen eyes beneath a broad-brimmed hat, and his moody and variable temperament, invested him with a strange personality. There was something approaching to genius in the man, but his life puzzled some and repelled others, and he died in comparative obscurity. During late years his fame as a writer has grown, and he has what may be described as a large following. He lived on the banks of Oulton Broad, and Fitz-Gerald saw him both at Yarmouth and Lowestoft, lent him Persian MSS., and gossiped about translation, but they were never very intimate.

Edward Fitz-Gerald

MARRIAGE OF EDWARD FITZ-GERALD AND LUCY BARTON.

The story of Fitz-Gerald's marriage has an element of the tragic. It was one of the many cases of incompatibility of habits and disposition, and was the result of solicitude apart from love. The drags were always on; when one did not apply them the other did, and the natural result followed. The marriage car came to a standstill, and neither occupant troubled to grease the wheels to promote harmony. Between him and his wife there was a certain intellectual, but no spiritual affinity. Their habits were dissimilar; each **was** eccentric. Marriage came at too late a period of life for either to begin on a new track, while a beginning was necessary in order to ensure smoothness

The Life of

of running of the domestic wheels. The truth is that, for reasons to be seen anon, Fitz-Gerald's compassion got the better of his judgment, and both had to suffer. Whatever the penalty, it was self-imposed, and was apparently borne with unrepining resignation. Of course it led to scandal, as such matters always do, but the whole thing was simple enough of explanation to those who knew both husband and wife.

Very little is publicly known as to the details of the marriage. Indeed, many people were unaware that he was married, and regarded him as an eccentric bachelor in the lucky possession of means, both to gratify and condone his whims. Misconception and glaring misstatements respecting his connection have so long prevailed that it is necessary, in justice to his memory, to enable the public to become better acquainted with the history of this momentous event in his life, leaving them to draw their own inferences.

Edward Fitz-Gerald

Bernard Barton and Edward Fitz-Gerald were for some years intimate friends; the acquaintance doubtless began soon after Fitz-Gerald's parents settled at Boulge Hall. After 1836 his letters to Barton are frequent and upon all sorts of subjects, showing great intimacy and close companionship. Thus—'To-morrow is Barton's birthday, and I am going to help him to celebrate it.'—'I only returned home a few days ago to spend Christmas with Barton, whose turkey I accordingly partook of.'—'Barton comes and sups with me to-morrow.' This intimacy ripened and continued till Barton's death.

Bernard Barton was a widower with one child, a daughter, who, having in infancy lost her mother, was brought up by her grandmother, with whom she lived until old enough to take charge of her father's home. From the time that she entered upon these responsibilities father and daughter were inseparables, and Lucy, who had great natural ability, became, under his fostering care, a woman of culture,[1] with a constant desire to improve her taste and enlarge her understanding. There was no Whittier in those days, and a poet among Quakers was so far an anomaly that Bernard Barton's accomplishments in that direction gained for him a degree of celebrity which he would not have achieved in any other religious circle. He was lionised in Woodbridge and its neighbourhood. Literary men and others of good position in society were fond of spending an hour or two with the Quaker poet, and the daughter, by mixing with them and presiding at her father's table, acquired the manners that enabled her to hold her own among all classes. Her natural ability was shown in other ways. On one occasion, when only a young woman, she accompanied her father to London to see Charles Lamb. In advanced years nothing pleased her better than to relate her reminiscences of

[1] See Letter from her in Appendix.

Edward Fitz-Gerald

this visit, which, besides being full of interest, was told in such a graphic and picturesque way as to excite the attention of all who were privileged to listen.

Having left the Society of Friends, to which all her family belonged, she became a member of the Church of England, and established a Bible class for lads, which she held every Sunday afternoon at her own house, where she was well known for her decision of character and ability to rule.

Her father's salary as bank clerk, his pension of one hundred pounds a year from the Civil List, and the income arising from the sale of his poems, enabled them to live in comparative ease and dispense hospitality to their friends. This income was abruptly diminished by the death of her father. She had a small property in her own right, but the rentals therefrom were insufficient to maintain her. To meet current expenses she sold the pictures and furniture, and by this means, and the publication of a volume

The Life of

of *Selections* from her father's poems, she met all requirements, and at the same time preserved her property. To this volume of *Selections* Edward Fitz-Gerald contributed a charming biography, and writing to his friend Frederick Tennyson, he mentions being engaged editing some of the Quaker poet's letters and poems, he having died, leaving his daughter, a noble woman, almost unprovided for, and we are getting up this volume by subscription.

After the lapse of some months she was engaged by Mr Hudson Gurney, of Keswick Hall, Norwich, to live in his house as chaperone and companion to two of his grandnieces who had lost their mother. None but a lady of good education and general culture, with a knowledge of society, could have creditably performed the duties of such a post, and for these Lucy Barton was eminently qualified. Eventually the elder sister married, but the Gurneys did not part with their chaperone until the time

Edward Fitz-Gerald

came when she set about making preparations for her marriage with Edward Fitz-Gerald. This was more than *seven* years after the death of her father. It was not a secret marriage, though it was celebrated at a distance from their own home, All Saints Church, Chichester, being selected for the performance of the ceremony, which occurred on the 4th of November 1856, when Lucy Barton was nearly fifty years of age. Chichester was doubtless chosen by Miss Barton because she had relatives living there, and it will be seen by the copy of the register of this marriage, which will be found in the Appendix, that several members of the family signed the register.

At present nothing is publicly known as to what brought about this marriage. Of courting in the ordinary sense of that term there seems to have been none. Unpublished letters of Fitz-Gerald's which I have seen simply refer to Miss Barton in friendly terms, the writer expressing at times great respect. Woodbridge gossips said that they were betrothed in the presence of Bernard Barton, but no evidence has been offered in support of that statement. Immediately after the death of Mrs Fitz-Gerald, a writer in the *Academy* gave some interesting notices of her life at Croydon, and, referring to her marriage, stated that Bernard Barton asked Fitz-Gerald to act as his executor, and look after his daughter's interests. He consented, but when the time came to carry out the task, he found himself so confronted by difficulties, and distressed by the small income of Lucy Barton, that he thought it his duty to propose marriage, and thus ensure for her circumstances of comfort. He did so, and she accepted him. This very plausible theory is unsupported by facts. There was no will! Bernard Barton died intestate in February 1849, and administration of his estate was granted to Lucy Barton on the 10th of the following April. The bonds were Richard Jones of

Edward Fitz-Gerald

Woodbridge, surgeon, and Abraham Brook of the same place, wine merchant. Edward Fitz-Gerald was not even one of the bonds.

Coleridge spent his honeymoon within sound of the sea, and Fitz-Gerald went to Brighton for the first few days of his married life. Removing to London, husband and wife lived in Great Portland Street for several weeks. It looks, however, as if the daily intercourse and domestic ties consequent upon marriage revealed traits of character from which misunderstandings arose, otherwise one can hardly suppose that a wife would absent herself from her husband for five consecutive weeks, on a visit to friends, during the first eleven weeks after her marriage. On January 22, 1857, Fitz-Gerald informed Professor Cowell that his wife had been five weeks in Norfolk, whilst he had been *alone* during that period at his old lodging in London. She returned the day before he penned this letter, and they took apartments in Portland Terrace,

Regent's Park, for two months. Apparently at this date he saw that separation must come, as he wished the professor to send letters for him to Bredfield Rectory till further directions. 'Till I see better how we get on, I dare fix on no place to live or die in.'

Their characters were in many ways so opposite that estrangement seemed to come naturally. Mrs Fitz-Gerald was careful to have everything in the house neat and orderly, and was prim and even fussy about her own and her husband's apparel. He on the other hand was careless alike as to dress and domestic arrangements. He was oblivious of the conventionalities of domestic life, and had lived too long as a solitary student, a bachelor and a Bohemian, to change his habits. There cannot be a doubt that to a woman so painfully punctilious as Lucy Barton, Edward Fitz-Gerald was a very trying man to deal with, but having known him intimately for seventeen years,

Edward Fitz-Gerald

it seems surprising that so clever a woman could have expected him to alter his mode of life. He was sad enough himself, could get no quietude, and longed for the company of Professor Cowell and his wife, who were living in Calcutta. He writes, 'My wife is sick of hearing me sing in a doleful voice the old glee, 'When shall we three meet again,' especially the stanza 'Though in foreign lands we sigh, parcht beneath a hostile sky, etc.' To these friends he made known his sad and miserable condition: 'I believe there are new channels fretted in my cheeks with my unmanly tears since I saw you, remembering the days that are no more, in which you two are so much mixt up.' Just imagine the miserable condition such a man as Edward Fitz-Gerald must have arrived at before he would have penned such sentences as these.

The difficulties of his wedded life increased, and it was not long after his lamentation to his friend Cowell was written that a separation was mutually agreed upon. As might be expected Fitz-Gerald behaved generously in the matter of allowance from his estate, and the deed was placed in the hands of trustees. Mrs Fitz-Gerald lived first at Hastings, then at Brighton, and finally at Croydon, enjoying through her husband's liberality every comfort that she needed. As she lived till she was ninety years of age, the separation would not appear to have seriously marred her happiness. The worst tragedy in life is a mistaken marriage. In such a case as Fitz-Gerald's, where it is believed he acted on a generous impulse, it was less wrong to agree to a separation than to continue living a life which must result in misery, not for one only, but for both.

Fitz-Gerald himself returned to Woodbridge, and lived at Farlingay Hall or at Bredfield Rectory. His return without his wife created gossip, and the female portion of the community were strong in their de-

Edward Fitz-Gerald

nunciations. Thus, a friend of Mrs Edward Fitz-Gerald's, writing to me just after the separation and referring to her said, 'if I must tell the unwelcome truth, she has now enough to bear from the atrocious proceedings of her husband, who is highly unprincipled or insane. She is now living at Hastings, he anywhere.' This is typical of the feeling then entertained towards Fitz-Gerald by a large number of the ladies of Woodbridge, and he frequently felt indignant at hearing remarks that were levelled at him, but he resolved to live down the gossip, and after a few months he returned to apartments (which he had formerly occupied) on the Market Hill, Woodbridge. His dearest friends remained true to him, as they were convinced that his marriage was the result of a generous impulse. It was in every way unwise, and he paid for his rashness by a lifelong penalty. My readers may rest assured that such a man as Archdeacon Groome, who lived on the spot, and knew all the circumstances, would have instantly dropped Fitz-Gerald from his list of friends, had he acted from unprincipled motives.

After a lapse of forty-years, a common-sense view of the case is more prevalent among women. During the last two years I have received the following from ladies who knew Fitz-Gerald and his wife well.

'Certainly that marriage was a mistake, both so clever, both so good and honourable, but neither fitted, I think, for married life. Each made to live alone, I should say, from peculiar disposition, good as they were. Clever people are not always the best in home life.'

Another says:—' She did not suit him, he provided for her well, and was anxious to treat her with proper respect, but Mr Fitz-Gerald was too long unmarried to adapt himself to anything but a single life.'

Some years may elapse before the evidence upon which to base a final judgment is

Edward Fitz-Gerald

made public, but those who still have faith in the translator of Omar Khayyám, need, I am convinced, have no fear that—

> 'Whatever record leap to light
> He never can be shamed.'

The Life of

LORD HOUGHTON AND 'LITTLE GRANGE.'

I must not pass without notice Fitz-Gerald's acquaintance with Richard Monckton Milnes, afterwards Lord Houghton, although but little trace of their friendship can be found in the Letters published by the editor of Fitz-Gerald's works. The biographer of Lord Houghton says, 'Edward Fitz-Gerald, the author of *Omar Khayyám*, had long been one of his correspondents, and in his later days Fitz-Gerald's letters took the place of those of some earlier friends, who had passed away.' He was a man of good culture, a poet of no mean powers, good-hearted and amiable in every way, was friendly with Carlyle, Spedding, Connop Thirlwall, and a host of literary and

Edward Fitz-Gerald

social dons. He was too much of a fashionable man of the world to be on very intimate terms with Fitz-Gerald. He liked to pose as a man of universal sympathies. Disraeli rather sarcastically observed of him, ' he was the Steward of Polish Balls, and the Vindicator of Russian humanity, he dined with Louis Phillippe, and gave dinners to Louis Blanc.' He had wealth at his back, and after he became M.P., his breakfasts at his London residence were renowned. He invited all classes of persons provided they were celebrated, that qualification was indispensable. He had travelled over Europe and America, and in the latter country made a number of friends, partook of the hospitality of Longfellow and Emerson, and renewed his acquaintance with Dr Robert Collyer, the Yorkshire blacksmith, who had established his fame as one of the greatest preachers in the United States. The shyness of Fitz-Gerald prevented him from joining Monckton Milnes' social circle. In

The Life of

the love of Keats and his poetry, they found a common bond of union, though they had very little intercourse after they left Cambridge, and in 1880 their correspondence had dwindled down to a yearly letter.

The following characteristic letters of Fitz-Gerald's are from the 'Life of Lord Houghton,' by Sir Wemyss Reid, and are inserted here by his kind permission:—

'*Market Hill, Woodbridge, April 8th,* 1872.

'DEAR LORD HOUGHTON,—It is rather hard to ask you to write about trifles, you have so much to write and do; but you have always been very obliging to me, and so here goes with my little business. I have just been reading your *Life and Letters of Keats*, for the second time, edition 1867, and I want to know who was the lady he died in love with, or if I may not know her name, whether she was single or married. Was she the "Charmian" Miss of p. 192? not the lady who said he looked "quite the

Edward Fitz-Gerald

little poet" to be sure; and by-the-bye, how tall was he? Above five feet surely, which he talks of in one place? I wonder Messrs Browning, Morris, Rossetti, &c. can read Keats' hastiest doggerel and not be ashamed at being trumpeted as great poets in the *Athenæum* and elsewhere. Only to mention Tennyson alone, to compare themselves with, who *used not* to think himself equal to Keats at all. I don't know what he thinks now, after so much worship has been offered him. To Keats he is not equal in invention and strength of continued flight, at any rate; but certainly farther above Browning & Co., than below his predecessor. I think *that Quarterly* should be printed along with the *Life of Keats*, as a warning to reviewers. I think you will excuse my troubling you. A very few words will answer me, and do not answer if not proper or agreeable.—Yours sincerely,

'E. Fitz-Gerald.'

To the same he says:—

'*April 12th*, 1872.

'I can care nothing for his (Tennyson's) poems, since his two volumes in 1842, except for the dramatic element in 'Maud,' and a few little bits in it—but I am told this is because I have shut up my mind, &c. So it may be. But surely he has become more artist than poet ever since, and the artist has not the wherewithal to work on. I mourn over him, as once a great man lost—that is, not risen to the greatness that was in him.'

'*Little Grange, Woodbridge, April* 30, 1878.

'DEAR LORD HOUGHTON,—You are, as ever, very kind to me, not least so in writing me a letter, which I find is a hard task to my oldest friends now, partly because of their being oldest I suppose. My dear old Spedding, I can barely screw out a dozen

Edward Fitz-Gerald

lines once a year from him. I have just had them, almost two months before the year was out, and on them I must try to live another year more.

"And with the aid such correspondents give
Life passes on—'tis labour—but we live."

'So says Crabbe, only "ships and sailing" in the first line, from his *Borough*, which with the rest of him no one now reads except myself, I believe. I write at once not only to thank you, but to return you Lushington's corrections. I should have thought they were printer's not copyist's errors. In return for all this, I enclose you one of my works. You see I drew it for myself, because I often find myself puzzled about the few dates in the dear fellow's life, when reading his letters, as they are now edited; then I thought thát some others would like such a "Cotelette d' Agneau a' la Minute" as Pollock calls it, and so here it is for you if you please. I

The Life of

am told that the present generation sneers at C. L. I suppose a natural revolt from their predecessors—*us* who love him so well. But his turn will come again, I feel sure. " Saint Charles," said old Thackeray to me in a third floor in Charlotte St., thirty years ago, putting one of C.L.'s letters to his forehead. I swear to the exact accuracy of my *Cotelette*, it is not easy to get it all from his biographies — and I am — Paddy, but I believe it is near enough. Pray do not be at the trouble of acknowledging it. You entertained many people at that 26 Pall Mall as I can witness for one, and one of us was a thief. I suppose some one stole a volume I had of Thackeray's drawings, which I lent to Annie T. when she was about that best *Orphan of Pimlico*. I entreated her to use some of his more graceful drawings, enough caricature already; but she or her publisher listened not, and she never could find my book again. I did not want it again, but I did not wish it to fall

Edward Fitz-Gerald

into other hands than hers. Now I think you have enough of Yours very sincerely,

'EDWARD.'

(How mány more of the name do you know?)

'FITZ-GERALD.'

'Surely the Keats should be published. What a fuss the cockneys make about Shelley just now; not worth Keats' little finger.'

The enclosure in Fitz-Gerald's letter was a brief list of the principal dates and events in Lamb's life, just such a list as would be found useful by any reader of his letters.

In the summer of 1864 Fitz-Gerald bought a small farmhouse in the outskirts of Woodbridge, which originally belonged to the 'Grange Farm' at Melton. This house he so altered and enlarged as to make it into a very agreeable, if not a convenient residence, but nearly nine years elapsed after the alterations before he went to live there. He was lodging with a Mr. Berry, a gunmaker, Market Hill, Woodbridge, and was very comfortable, until his landlord took unto himself a second wife. Fitz-Gerald was not in the habit of mincing his words, and the lady, hearing him make use of an expression which greatly reflected on her, she requested her husband to give him notice to quit. This was done, but to give Fitz-Gerald this notice must have been a hard pill for Mr. Berry to swallow, because, as a lodger, he was one of a thousand. He never rang the bell for the servant to wait upon him if he could avoid it. He would leave his lodgings for weeks at a time, but his rent was paid just the same. On one occasion he went to stay at Aldeburgh for a week, simply because the servant had left, and he wished the new hand to get used to the place before she had the trouble of seeing after his two rooms. To obtain the

Edward Fitz-Gerald

necessary provisions for him, Fitz-Gerald would hand Mr. Berry a £5 note, saying, 'Tell me when it is all spent.'

When he left Mr. Berry he was undecided as to his future movements. Although he could have moved at once to 'Little Grange,' he hired a room next door to the gunmaker's, and wrote to a friend, 'I have been bothered in a small way about moving, and have literally seen my things all crushed into a little room. Whether I shall have courage to begin housekeeping again remains to be proved. Meanwhile, I am here at my own house, which I always wished to keep for my nieces.'

In 'Little Grange,' however, he ultimately settled, and soon found that, however pleasant it was to see one's gables and chimneys occupy a place in the landscape, yet he had indulged in an expensive luxury. He also discovered that the altered house, after costing him nearly double what he had anticipated, 'is just what I do not want,

The Life of

according to the usage of the Bally blunder family, of which I am a legitimate offspring.' A dining-room and an entrance hall were added to the old farmhouse, but these additions belonged to a part of the house which he reserved principally for his nieces from Geldeston, who took possession for two or three months in the summer of every year. A large room, which he called study, was built for his own use. This was divided, and had folding doors. One of these divisions he used for his meals and for reading and writing. Pens, ink, paper, and paste were there in abundance, and near the window was a desk on high legs with a drawer under the sloping top; at this he stood and did his writing. The other division was used as a bedroom, in which was a folding bed. Each of these rooms was lined with book shelves, and it looked sometimes as if books were the chief article of furniture. This one room, he said, 'serves for parlour, bedroom, and all. And it does very well

Edward Fitz-Gerald

for me, reminding me of my former cabin life in my little ship.'

The chairs and tables in these rooms were simply useful, no extra expense had been incurred in their purchase; but in that part of the house used by his nieces the furniture was both elegant and substantial. Antique cabinet inlaid with mother-of-pearl, handsome carved work table, carved smoking-chair, antique carved oak cabinet with drawers, met the eye. In fact nothing was spared that would render these rooms attractive. Relics of Thomas Carlyle and parson Crabbe were placed on a table. A number of drawings by Churchyard and others hung on the walls, alongside of which were pictures of a more important character, including portraits of Alfred Tennyson, Archdeacon Allen, Crabbe the poet, and a crayon drawing of Thackeray. He had also a fine landscape by Titian, 'Abraham and Isaac,' and a portrait of Raphael Mengs. He was one day very pleased when a London

The Life of

picture-dealer, who was hunting about Suffolk for pictures by Old Crome, called upon him, and seeing the landscape by Titian, said, 'that ought to be in the National Gallery.' Fitz-Gerald told him he had bequeathed it to the Fitz-William Museum at Cambridge, upon which he said, 'a very proper place for it.' Fitz-Gerald, when speaking of 'Old Crome,' said, 'I think he falls far short of the Dutchmen. Like the Dutchmen I find his sketches better than his finished pictures, but this is not the fashionable opinion.'

On the staircase leading to the drawing-room there was a cast of Woolner's bust of Tennyson—the marble is in the library of Trinity College, Cambridge. Of this cast an incident was related to me by Captain Woolner which is worth putting on record. A few months after the death of Fitz-Gerald, the Suffolk sculptor, Thomas Woolner, R.A., was staying with his brother, Captain Woolner, at Hintlesham,

Edward Fitz-Gerald

and they went to Ipswich, six miles distant, looking about for anything interesting. They wandered as far as Fore Street, when the sculptor stopped at a small shop where books, pictures, and curios were exposed for sale. He was looking at the window, when the Captain said, 'I don't think you will find anything there, Tom,' and he replied, 'You don't know that, you may find something anywhere. Ha! look there!' The captain looked in the direction indicated, and saw a plaster cast of his brother's bust of Tennyson. The sculptor said, 'I know that cast well; it is the only one that I cleaned the seams off myself,' alluding to the ridges at the junction of the different pieces of the mould. 'I charged £5, 5s. for a cast of that bust, the seams being cleaned off by my assistants, but Fitz-Gerald offered to give me double the price if I would clean off the seams myself. Poor dear old Fitz; I did not like to refuse him, and so I did it. He sent me his cheque for

£10, 10s., but, busy as I was just then, it was a serious inroad into my time, and £200 would not more than have paid me.' The captain asked, 'Do you want it?' and he replied, 'not if you do; if not, of course I shall buy it.' They went into the shop, and after asking the price of various things, the captain carelessly looked at the bust and said, 'What is that?' 'Oh! that's a bust I bought at the sale of Mr. Fitz-Gerald of Boulge.' 'Who is it?' 'Oh, I don't know.' 'Who is it by?' 'A man named, let's see, who is it? Oh, here you are; Thomas Woolner,' pointing to the cut inscription at the side, 'that's it. Thomas Woolner, London, lives in the New Road, I think' (a locality famous for sculptors of the tombstone kind). 'How much? I have taken a house at Holbrook, and it would do for the hall or staircase, so how much? Delivered at Holbrook? But it must be cheap.' The dealer considered, and said, 'Well, it takes up a lot of room, and no one

Edward Fitz-Gerald

seems to fancy it; say a sovereign.' 'All right,' said the captain, 'but it must be delivered safely.' 'I will undertake that,' said the dealer, and the brothers left the shop. As soon as he recovered from laughing, the sculptor said, I think you have made an uncommonly good bargain!'

A French casement in Fitz-Gerald's study opened into a garden which had an abundance of sweet-scented common flowers. Roses, white and red, sweet williams, wallflowers, heartsease, pinks, and many other old-fashioned flowers, with scarcely anything that could be called choice. He had a great love of colour, and obtained it without being what is called a good customer of the florist's. Outside the French casement was his favourite walk, which he called his 'Quarter Deck.' This was suffused at certain seasons with the fragrance of cloves and mignonette, the flowers being allowed to wander and grow as nature meant them, or at their own sweet will.

VISITS OF FRIENDS, OLD AND NEW.

Tennyson at Woodbridge.

The year 1871 was memorable to FitzGerald as that in which he sold his yacht. Throughout life he had been very fond of the sea, and after his eyesight was almost extinguished, it became his one great source of enjoyment; his love of boating was nearly a passion. Whenever he stayed at Lowestoft or Aldeburgh, he was a rare good customer to the boatmen. In 1863, a small yacht was built for him, which cost £360, and as soon as she was afloat, he invited friends, one or two at a time, to make short trips with him round the Norfolk or the Sussex coasts. He was always trying to get away from the distractions of the world, and during several summers and autumns,

Edward Fitz-Gerald

he lived almost entirely on the element he loved so well.

Being a good sailor, he liked a voyage best with a rough sea, and accompanied by a Woodbridge friend, he once undertook to make a trip to Holland in the month of August. He went rushing about to Rotterdam and Amsterdam, but saw nothing he cared for, having missed The Hague Gallery of Pictures. Thus disappointed, the stench of the muddy canals was too much for him, and he tore back to Bawdsey Ferry as fast as his yacht would bring him, declaring that he would never go abroad again. This resolution, however, was broken. When cruising about Ramsgate with his brother Peter, he sailed for Calais, just to touch French soil, drink a bottle of French wine, and then home. This trip pleased him, as it brought strongly to his remembrance the France of his childhood. Oft-times he lived in his little ship for weeks, with no company but his crew of two men, and one year he stayed there so late in the season that sleeping two nights in his cold cabin nearly laid him up. About the welfare of his small crew he was very considerate. When on a cruise he invariably ran for a port on a Sunday, not through any regard for the sanctity of the day, but that his sailors might go ashore for a hot dinner; and when he laid up his yacht for the winter (which he called shutting up shop), he regaled them with a Michaelmas goose. A peculiarity to note is that he would frequently stop short of the place for which he started, and suddenly put about and return home.

He maintained that the sea quickened his appetite for Greek. One day when sailing in a friend's yacht, he was jerked overboard by a sudden jib. He was calmly scanning a Greek play at the time, and when he was fished aboard the book was in his hand, and he quietly resumed his reading, after declining a change of clothes which

Edward Fitz-Gerald

was offered by his companions. 'No harm, said he, 'could arise from a ducking in salt water.'[1]

To part with his yacht because he could not see to read in the cabin of his 'dear little ship' was, as may readily be supposed, a terrible blow to him, and he did not hesitate to say, that in giving up sea trips, he should be consigned once more to 'cold, indoor, solitude, melancholy, and ill health.'

As the years rolled on the infirmities of age became more manifest, though at this date he was by no means an old man. His eyes had long been so inflamed that he wrote as little as possible; at this time his letters were in red ink, and one year he used a black lead pencil, remarking that anything is better than a steel pen. At the commencement of 1872, he said he had read *nothing* for months till the last fortnight, when he began to nibble at some books from Hookham's. He had scarce 'been

---

[1] Layard's *Life of Charles Keene.*

The Life of

away from home all last year because of these eyes, which would not let me read in a lodging when I had nothing else to do, whereas here at home I can potter about my house and garden, feed the chickens, and play with the cat.' This monotonous kind of life made him querulous, and sometimes full of lamentations. 'No new books, no new pictures, no new music,' he cried, but he refrained from going where he might have seen and heard about all these, because he feared to strain his eyes. He had lost all curiosity as to what might be seen or heard in London. Of the world he knew little beyond what a stray newspaper told him, as he had hardly been out of Suffolk for a dozen years, and in a melancholy tone, he would say his day was done. His solitary habits had told upon him greatly, and he was conscious that mixing in society, or going to see his friends, was the only cure; but he had lost the taste for this so long that he could not endure it again.

Edward Fitz-Gerald

Poring over Persian MSS. by the aid of a lamp till midnight, which he had done for months in succession, had injured his eyesight, and this took away the power of reading, which was the joy of his life.

Thus troubled, he resolved to employ boy readers, and one of these read to him the whole of the Tichborne trial, in which he was absorbed. He was very fond of Trollope's novels, but admitted that the Tichborne case had fascinated him more. He must have been fond of criminal trials, as he speaks of visits to the Ipswich assizes as among his great treats, and his library contained the trials of Thistlewood, Thurtell, Manning, Rush, Palmer, Burke, and a host of other murderers, bound in seven volumes, profusely illustrated with portraits and views. He had to change his reader, as the lad made so many blunders, and whilst staying at Lowestoft he wrote to a Woodbridge friend to find ' either a lad or a lout, who will help me to get through the

The Life of

long winter evenings, whether by cards or reading.' A lad was found who was a much better reader than the first one, who enjoyed something of what he read, and could laugh heartily, and then matters went on smoothly. The engagement continued for three years, and the hours were 7.30 to 9.30 p.m. The young fellow knew the value of time, and Fitz-Gerald, to compliment him on his punctuality, called him 'the ghost.' Pleased by the title, the lad very often stood outside the gate, waiting till the stroke of the church clock for the half-hour faded into silence, before he rapped at the door.

The first hour was devoted to the reading of articles from *Chambers's Journal, All the Year Round, Cornhill*, and other magazines. Then they adjourned to the little pantry for supper, which consisted of bread and cheese, radishes, milky puddings, or plum cake, and as the lad was an abstainer, fruit essence was provided as a beverage, whilst he mixed for himself a glass of grog.

Edward Fitz-Gerald

They always helped themselves, to prevent the housekeeper or her husband being disturbed. Then back to the sitting-room, when came what he called 'the *pièce de resistance*,' which was ofttimes a novel of Scott's or Dickens'. Sometimes a book of travel was selected, and one winter *Pepys' Diary*, in six or eight volumes, was gone through. When he was in ordinary health, it was a pleasure to read to him, but when he suffered from an attack of gout, he was very difficult to please, and applied hard words sometimes to reader and author. But if he had been extra cutting in his remarks, he would either apologise to the lad, or, as he said, 'insult him in a pecuniary manner.'

He always sat in a high-backed, low-seated, red-covered armchair, often in dressing-gown and slippers, and invariably kept his hat on, which seemed never to be removed except when he wanted a red handkerchief from the interior. Two wax

The Life of

candles were used for lighting the table. He sat with his feet on the fender, holding in his hand either a paper knife or his snuff box. If interested in what was read, he sat very still, making but little comment, but slightly fidgetting his beard with his paper knife; but when not interested, he took snuff frequently, and shifted about uneasily, and if annoyed, he requested his reader emphatically to pass that d——d rot. He never smoked whilst the reading was going on, but as soon as it was finished, he would take a new long clay pipe from a drawer, and fill it. The same pipe was not used more than once, as he always broke it after the tobacco was consumed, and the pieces were thrown into the fender.

This young reader says: 'I remember one evening finding him in a very perturbed state of mind, having mislaid his spectacles, and when I asked him if I could help him in any way, he petulantly exclaimed, "Oh, no! it is just about the way I shall get

Edward Fitz-Gerald

to heaven, searching for what I can't find." '

At the opening of this period his prospects were gloomy, but consolations in the shape of friendships gained and friendships renewed were in store for him, among which not the least valued was the beginning of his correspondence with Fanny Kemble. These 'Letters' began in 1871, and were continued with unfailing regularity till within a fortnight of his decease. The two friends had known each other from childhood, and this series of letters form almost an autobiography of Fitz-Gerald during the period named, as he gossiped on all kinds of things, and of persons also who were known to his friend, and they included a considerable number of friends who were also well known to himself: Miss Thackeray, Tennyson, Carlyle, Spedding, W. B. Donne, and others.

Fitz-Gerald was eccentric; Fanny Kemble was peculiar. She was a good correspondent, but was guided by rules that were as rigid as the laws of the Medes and Persians. In a letter to a friend, she says, 'You bid me not answer your letter, but I have certain organic laws of correspondence, from which nothing short of a miracle causes me to depart, as for instance, I never write till I am written to, I always write when I am written to, and I make a point of always returning the same amount of paper I receive.' Fitz-Gerald wrote to her once a month, the time fixed being the full moon, and no matter whether she was in Italy, France, Switzerland, America, or England, his letter was regularly despatched, though when the lady was on the Continent, he sometimes had to forward it to 'Coutts,' the London bankers, with a request that they would add the address. His great regard for Fanny Kemble may be measured by the fact that she was the only person to whom he wrote on his birthday. Fitz-Gerald hated Browning's poetry, and was

Edward Fitz-Gerald

pleased that, when solicited, she declined to become a member of the Browning Society.

Fitz-Gerald was cheered in the middle of May 1872, by a visit from Mr. W. F. Pollock—a son of Sir Frederick Pollock—one of the most regular of his correspondents, with whom he had been on intimate terms ever since their college days. Mr. Pollock was one of the contributors to *Fraser's Magazine*, was fond of the drama, and had a good knowledge of music and pictures, so that they had much in common to gossip about. Fitz-Gerald had about eight years previously purchased the house he afterwards called 'Little Grange,' and expended a considerable sum of money in alterations, but he still remained in his lodgings over a gunsmith's shop, on the Market Hill, Woodbridge, his nieces having possession of the newly arranged house. Mr. Pollock says, 'he put me up at his own charge at the principal inn. No man who has deserved so much fame for his writings, was probably ever so modest and retiring. Our talk was chiefly of old days and old friends, J. M. Kemble, Thackeray, Spedding, Thompson, and others. In the neighbourhood he is regarded as a benevolent oddity.'

One morning in the month of September Fitz-Gerald's aged housekeeper brought him a visiting card, on which he read with surprise and delight—

MR ALFRED TENNYSON,
FARRINGFORD.

Across this was written, in pencil, 'Dear Old Fitz, I am passing through and will call again.' Instead of calling again, Tennyson followed the housekeeper into Fitz-Gerald's room, and his hearty greeting announced his presence. The two friends, who had not met for twenty years, were at once so absorbed in the pleasure of meeting that it seemed as if their absence from each other had not been more than twenty days. The poet's eldest son Hallam was with him.

Edward Fitz-Gerald

They had been a tour in the district, and diverged a little from the ordinary route in order to give 'Old Fitz' a call, and he seemed almost as pleased with the unpretending manners of the son, as he was with the old stories, and pictures of old times, and old friends which were vividly and fluently rehearsed by the father. He said Tennyson looked much the same, the loss of some of his flowing locks excepted. As his own house was not in a fit condition to receive the unexpected guests, he put them up at the chief hotel in Woodbridge, 'The Bull,' feeling sure that the landlord, John Grout, would take care that everything of the best was provided for his friends. The next day Fitz-Gerald took them to Ipswich for a trip by steamer down the charming river Orwell, the banks of which had much to delight the poet's eye. Tennyson stayed two days with his old friend, at the end of which they parted at the railway station to see each other no more.

The Life of

A humorous incident occurred in connection with this visit. When the poet and his son got out of the train, Tennyson asked one of the porters to direct him to the residence of Mr. Edward Fitz-Gerald. It so happened that a Mr. Edward Blood Fitz-Gerald was at that time stationed at Woodbridge as superintendent of the county police of the district, and as he was much better known to the railway staff than was the translator of Omar, the poet laureate and his son were directed to the home of the superintendent in Seckford Street. When they reached the house the mistake of the railway porter was discovered, and superintendent Fitz-Gerald kindly escorted the travellers to 'Little Grange,' where the eccentric Edward Fitz-Gerald was found. This was probably the first and last time that the poet laureate was escorted to a friend's house by a policeman.

Lord Tennyson has kindly permitted me to quote from his *Life of the Poet Laureate*.

Edward Fitz-Gerald

He says, 'Fitz-Gerald's vegetarianism interested my father, and he was charmed by the picture of the lonely philosopher, a man of humorous melancholy mark, with his grey floating locks, sitting among his doves, which perched about on head and shoulders and knees, and cooed to him as he sat in the sunshine beneath his roses.'

Again, 'In September 1876, my father and I visited Fitz-Gerald at Woodbridge. He was affectionate, genial, and humorous, declaring that the captain of his lugger was one of the greatest of men. The views that Fitz-Gerald expressed to me on literature were original and interesting, but the old man never got off his own platform to look at the work of modern authors. He had always wanted men like Thackeray and my father to go along with his crotchets, which were many. He had not been carried away by their genius out of himself, and out of his own Cambridge critical groove; and had not, like them, grown with the times.' After we had arrived home he wrote :—

'Woodbridge, September 26th, 1876.

'I am glad you were pleased with your short visit here. Perhaps you will one day, one or both of you, come again, and if you will but give me warning, and no nieces are in possession of the house, it shall be ready for you, and some *tender* meat provided. Somehow I, when you were gone, felt somewhat abroad, and a few hours after went to an old village by the sea, Dunwich, once a considerable town, now swept into the sea, with the remains of a church on the cliff, and the walls of a priory beside. I was wishing that I had made you come with me, over a stretch of wild heath too, but there was no room in the little inn, and, I daresay, *very tough meat!* That fatal reed sticks in my side you see! But I am still yours and all yours sincerely,

'E. F. G.

Edward Fitz-Gerald

Tennyson, when he published 'Tiresias' and other poems, exhibited to the world his regard for Edward Fitz-Gerald by dedicating the volume to him, as an old and much loved friend. In this dedication he thus affectionately addressed him :—

> '*Old Fitz*, who from your suburb grange
>   Where once I tarried for a while,
> Glance at the wheeling orb of change,
>   And greet it with a kindly smile;
> Whom yet I see as there you sit
>   Beneath your sheltering garden tree,
> And watch your doves about you flit,
>   And plant on shoulder, hand, and knee,
> Or on your head their rosy feet,
>   As if they knew your diet spares,
> Whatever moved in that full sheet
>   Let down to Peter at his prayers;
> Who live on milk, and meal, and grass.'

This dedication was never seen by Fitz-Gerald. It was written only a short time before his decease, when the friendship of the two men had lasted nearly half a century, but the hand of death removed the Woodbridge recluse before the publication of the volume. The dedication was intended as a birthday commemoration, which Tennyson said he knew his friend would welcome

> 'Less for its own than for the sake
>   Of one recalling gracious times,
> When in our younger London days
>   You found some merit in my rhymes
> And I more pleasure in your praise.'

Dr. Johnson says if a man does not make new acquaintances as he advances through life, he will very soon find himself alone. Determined recluse as he was, Fitz-Gerald nevertheless sometimes acted upon this aphorism of Johnson's. The ruined city of Dunwich, five or six miles from Southwold, was a favourite seaside resort of his during the summer months. It was lonely, desolate, and very exclusive. Its extent and population were far below that of many villages in its immediate neighbourhood, yet at that time it was a municipal borough. There was only one public-house and one lodging-house in the place, and Fitz-Gerald took

Edward Fitz-Gerald

care to secure the apartments there. On one of these occasions he found a gentleman in broken health occupying a cottage which he had bought, hoping that sea air in summer and autumn would improve his condition. This was Edwin Edwards, a London artist, who took to painting late in life, and was afterwards better known by his etchings of 'Old Inns' than by his work on canvas. Fitz-Gerald and he soon became friendly, and, Mrs Edwards being a capital companion, he found himself thoroughly enjoying their society, and anxiously looking forward to their annual meetings at Dunwich. One year he lent them 'Little Grange' for a month, and Edwards set about teaching him Spanish dominoes. On one of these annual visits Edwards had a more acute attack, and hastily returned to London, and a few weeks put an end to his sufferings. Fitz-Gerald found the place too solitary without them, and moved on to Lowestoft. He visited the sufferer on his

The Life of

deathbed, and afterwards went to London to see the widow, but he never more took lodgings at Dunwich.

During one of these visits to Dunwich, Fitz-Gerald made the acquaintance of Charles Keene, one of the artists on *Punch*, who was staying with Mr and Mrs Edwin Edwards, and was so pleased with his company that he invited him to Woodbridge, and renewed the invitation every year. In many ways Keene was just the man to be a fitting companion for 'Old Fitz.' In eating and drinking Keene was very abstemious; he was a lover of music—mostly of old music,—and was well versed in quaint old English literature. This taste of his explains in some degree the rapidity with which his intimacy with Fitz-Gerald ripened. He had a quiet, humorous way with him, and, like Fitz-Gerald, was very shy among strangers, but lighted up immensely among friends. All through his life he was very much at peace with dust and cobwebs, and

Edward Fitz-Gerald

was fond of sitting in a room amid a chaos of old things, pictures, books, &c. He was a great smoker, and always used a short old fashioned little clay, which being small of bowl frequently needed refilling. He was careless in dress, did not mince his words, and paid no extra respect to a black cloth suit. When going on a holiday, he carried a very small portmanteau, which was made to contain all the luggage that he needed for a fortnight.[1] This is a fair description of the last man that Fitz-Gerald added to his list of friends.

Keene's description of Fitz-Gerald runs thus:—'At Dunwich there was an old *literato*, who had the only lodging in the place. He was quite a character, an Irishman, an author and bookworm, who remembered Kean and the Kembles and Liston, and was full of talk about old times, and dead and gone people. We met every evening, and talked *belles lettres*, Shake-

---

[1] Layard's *Life of Keene*.

speare, and the musical glasses till midnight.' In another letter he says, 'Old Fitz-Gerald is an eccentric old fellow; they think him daft at Woodbridge, but he's just one of our sort, very bookish, and fond of art and delightful company. . . . He is a great admirer of Bewick, and has a lot of proofs, and a block or two given him, I think, by Barnes of Durham. He's a great scholar, and a slashing critic about pictures; his taste is for the old masters, and he knew all the literary men about town in Thackeray's early time, a friend of Tennyson's and of Tom Carlyle the Diogenes of Chelsea.'

Again, June 1881, 'I went to stay with my old friend Fitz-Gerald at Woodbridge, and find since I've been back that he is a great unknown genius in some high critical circles. I was mentioning my visits to W. B. Scott, who is one of Rossetti's, Swinburne, &c., set, and of my friend having translated some Persian poems and

Edward Fitz-Gerald

Calderon's Plays, &c. He jumped off his chair! "Do you know him? Why **Ram Jam** (some wonderful Persian name he gave it) is the most exquisite work of the age, and **Rossetti** considers the translation from Calderon **the** finest thing," &c.'

Fitz-Gerald writing to Fanny Kemble, May 1881, says, 'And now my house is being pulled about my ears by preparation for my nieces next week, I believe that Charles Keene will be here from Friday to Monday. As he has long talked of coming, I do not like to put him off now that he has really proposed to come, and we shall scramble on somehow. I will get a carriage, and take him a long drive into the country where it is greenest.'

May 29th, 1882, 'I have Charles Keene staying Whitsuntide with me, and was to have had Archdeacon Groome to meet him, but he is worn out with Archidiaconal Charges and cannot come, but C. K. and I have been out in carriage to the sea, and no visitors nor host could wish for finer weather.'

May 1883, 'Next week I am expecting my grave friend Charles Keene of *Punch* to come for a week, bringing with him his bagpipes, and a book of Madrigals, and our Archdeacon will come to meet him and to talk ancient music and books, and we three shall drive out past the green hedges and heaths, with their furze in blossom—and I wish—yes I do, that you were of the party.'

May 27th, 1883, he says to his friend, 'I have had Charles Keene staying with me for ten days. He is a very good guest, inasmuch as he entertains himself with books and birds' nests, and also his bagpipes—his favourite instrument.' Late in the evening, Keene used to go into FitzGerald's garden to blow away at his bagpipes, to the great astonishment of the yokels, who were passing by, who did not, however, admire the music.

Edward Fitz-Gerald

The Rev. R. C. M. Rouse, who was for many years Rector of Woodbridge, writes me: 'Fitz-Gerald, as you know, was very much of a recluse, so that I saw him very occasionally. One of the most enjoyable afternoons I ever spent was when I went with Archdeacon Groome, who was staying with me, to call on him. Keene, the artist (on the *Punch* staff), was staying with him, and it certainly was an intellectual treat such as I have not often enjoyed. On leaving, E. F. G. said "Mr Rouse, don't forget to come with the Archdeacon the next time he comes to see me," and it was not long after that, he and I attended his funeral.'

In the early part of the year 1881 Fitz-Gerald experienced one of the severest shocks that he had felt during the whole of his life. This was news, that his friend Spedding had been knocked down and run over by a cab, and so seriously injured that he was taken at once to St George's Hospital, where he died, his injuries being

The Life of

so severe that the doctors would not risk his being removed to his home. His death was a terrible blow to Fitz-Gerald. His anxiety about 'Dear Old Jem' was so great, that as soon as he heard of the accident, he wrote to a friend asking that a post card might be sent to him daily with a word or two only on it thus—'better'—'less well,' or whatever it might be. Spedding was the man with whom among his dearest friends Fitz-Gerald had the greatest affinity. The friendship of these two men began at school, and lasted nearly sixty years, although during the latter part of their lives half-yearly letters were the extent of their correspondence, and when Spedding died, the two friends had not seen each other for twenty years. To Professor Norton, Fitz-Gerald wrote, 'He was the wisest man I have known, a Socrates in Life and in Death. . . . There was no one I loved and honoured more.'

Whilst staying at Aldeburgh in the autumn of 1882, Fitz-Gerald accidentally

Edward Fitz-Gerald

got into friendly relations with the well-known blind Professor Henry Fawcett. The Professor, in 1867, married Milicent, daughter of Mr Newson Garret of Aldeburgh, and whilst on one of his annual visits to his father-in-law he heard that Mr Aldis Wright of Cambridge was staying in the place with Fitz-Gerald. He called upon his friend, and the professor was so pleased with the conversation he had with the Persian scholar that he embraced an opportunity after A. W. had departed to spend an evening with Fitz-Gerald, who was as much surprised at the robust appearance and fine presence of the blind statesman, as he was delighted to hear his genial and hearty laugh. He also rejoiced to find that the Professor was a good smoker, for nothing pleased Fitz-Gerald more than to have an evening gossip, whilst both parties puffed away at tobacco. Fitz in writing to Fanny Kemble directly after the event says, 'I have made a new acquaintance,' and described him as a 'thoroughly unaffected, unpretending man; so modest indeed that I was ashamed afterwards to think how I had harangued him all the evening, instead of getting him to instruct me. But I would not ask him about his Parliamentary shop, and I should not have understood his political economy, and I believe he was very glad to be talked to instead, about some of those he knew, and some I had known. And as we were in Crabbe's Borough, we talked of him. The Professor, who had never read a word, I believe, about him, or of him, was pleased to hear a little, and I advised him to buy the Life, written by Crabbe's son, and I would give him my abstract of the *Tales of the Hall* by way of giving him a taste of the poet's self.'[1]

Mrs. Fawcett, writing to me of this interview, says—'I did not accompany my husband when he spent the evening with Fitz-Gerald in 1882, and I have no distinct

[1] Fitz-Gerald's *Letters to Fanny Kemble.*

Edward Fitz-Gerald

recollection of what my husband said about him on his return, except that they had had a very interesting conversation. On one occasion, I think also in 1882, my daughter went with her father to call on Mr. Fitz-Gerald when he was at Aldeburgh. Mr. Fitz-Gerald asked her what books she liked best. She replied, "Thackeray's and George Eliot's." He exclaimed, "What can your mother be thinking of to let you read such books?" He gave my husband *Readings from Crabbe* and *Crabbe's Life and Letters* as a souvenir of his visit.'

There was but little variation as to habits during the last ten years of his life. He was wearily resting even from those things which had interested and fascinated him for years, not from choice, but from compulsion. His eyes still troubled him greatly. He frequently could not bear the light from sun or lamp without wearing odious blue spectacles, which he could only discard when looking on grass or green leaves.

Even in his own garden he walked about with a green shade over his eyes. Exceptions he had, as he notes that after a stroll in his garden one evening by moonlight, shoes kicked off and slippers and dressing-gown on, he went in to try a letter to his friend Pollock. This improvement of his eyes was brought about by careful nursing, but when so improved, it was not long before he ventured on boating under a glaring sun, and thus he soon put his eyes out of *kelter* again.

In 1877 his old boatman, West, died. He had employed him more than a dozen years, and after the loss of his services he did not seem to have the heart to make his customary trips on the Deben. His solitary disposition increased. He gave up most of his house during the summer and autumn of each year to the use of his nieces, but, he said, 'they make but little change in my own way of life.' They live by themselves, and I only see them now and then in the

Edward Fitz-Gerald

garden, sometimes not five minutes in the day.' He frequently went to Lowestoft, either to lounge on the shore or to meet friends who were staying there. In the morning he might be seen chatting with Lord Hatherley on the esplanade, or walking on the pier with Dean Merivale or Dr. Thompson, the master of Trinity College, Cambridge, and in the evening he would be smoking a pipe on the bowling green of the Suffolk Hotel, with the late captain of his lugger or one of his crew. He did not like adverting to his own ailments; but of one of his visits to Lowestoft he writes—'I am going myself to meet the Cowells at Lowestoft; not very well myself, and (as I tell him) not so alert in mind or body as when we met there nine years ago. But I must do my best, and may find the change do me good, though I a little dread leaving my seclusion for company even of those I love so well. I feel that a very little company goes a long way now.' On a later occasion he spent ten days at Lowestoft, having Professor Cowell and his wife as neighbours. 'We had two or three hours of Don Quixote's company of a morning, and only ourselves for company at night.' These friends did more than any others to make the evening of Fitz-Gerald's life comfortable, whenever they had the opportunity of so doing.

Edward Fitz-Gerald

HIS LAST DAYS.

The last year of Fitz-Gerald's life opened, as far as health was concerned, more favourably than many of its predecessors. The early months were mild, and he told his friends that he had not much to complain of on the score of health. He had escaped any severe attack of bronchitis, from which he had suffered more or less during many winters. He got through the sunless days and the east winds of March pretty well, and his letters of this date show that he wrote with a firmer hand, and exhibited signs of improved condition. He was troubled at times by pains about the region of the heart, but he had learned from his doctor that this was one of the ills which he had to bear for the rest of his life.

Nevertheless, the infirmities of age crept on, bringing signs of the approaching end. The bend of the limbs, the loss of elasticity in his step, the curvature of the neck, occasional dimness of sight, and failing memory, were admonitions that his work was nearly done, that the hour would soon strike for his final rest. He told his friends that he began to 'smell the ground,' as sailors say of the ship that slackens speed when the water shallows under her. He frequently alluded to the sudden death of his mother, and said that members of his family rarely lived beyond seventy. He did not wish for long life, still less for a lingering death; wise man that he was, he learnt to anticipate the inevitable with tranquillity. One thing he hoped, that he should not live on with impaired faculties; thankfulness was in his heart when he wrote that he had only bronchitis to trouble him, whilst several of his friends had recently suffered from attacks of paralysis.

Edward Fitz-Gerald

When May arrived he felt himself well enough to undertake a journey to London, a place, above all, that he hated. Moreover, he had to go on disagreeable business. This over, he paid visits to the statue of his old friend Carlyle, on the Chelsea embankment, and to the house in Cheyne Row. With the statue he was pleased, but said that the environment spoilt the effect it might have produced; it wanted a good background to set it off. He had not seen Carlyle's home for nearly a quarter of a century, and as this might be his last visit to London he resolved to take one last look at the old house in which he had smoked many a pipe, drank many a cup of tea, and enjoyed many discussions with his old friend. But a shock was in store for him. When the cabman stopped at No. 5 Cheyne Row he found the house not only shut up and uninhabited, but wearing an utterly neglected appearance, whilst a board, *To Let*, stared him in the face.

The Life of

This was too much for him. He thought of the pains Mrs. Carlyle had taken to make this home attractive to her husband's friends, men and women from all parts of the world, who called to see the Chelsea sage, and now to see it covered with dirt, and with weeds growing abundantly in front, was a scene that disgusted him, and he got away from it, and from London also, as quickly as he could, and settled himself in his own dull home.

Fortunately, he was soon cheered by receiving the promise of a visit from Charles Keene. During the last years of his life, when most of his dearest friends were lost to him by death, when he could read little, and walking was an effort, he sat almost every evening smoking in his room, and having knocked the white ashes out of his pipe, the smoke from which had been curling in brave wreaths to the ceiling two minutes before, he could not, whenever a neighbour called in, conceal his longing for

Edward Fitz-Gerald

a letter giving news of his friends. Lord Tennyson was now almost the only one left, out of that early batch, to whom he clung as Jonathan did to David. So anxious was he to see his face that a year or two previous he had written, 'are you ever coming this way again?' And only two months before his death he pathetically wrote to the son, Hallam (now Lord Tennyson), 'It is now six months since I heard of you all, so be a good boy, and write me just enough to tell me how it fares with mother and father and all your party.'

Keene came, and brought with him his bagpipes. Fitz-Gerald was quite jubilant at the prospect of his company, and his love of nature was cheered at the chance of a drive to Dunwich, which would give him a good view of the country at the zenith of its spring-tide glory, when the furze was in full bloom, and all nature appeared to be rejoicing.

Fitz-Gerald always derived much pleasure from his visit to his friend Crabbe. In-

The Life of

dependent of the bond of friendship which bound him to the rector and his sisters, the village itself had many attractions for him. Less change had been made there than in Suffolk parishes. The hand of modern improvement was not visible; he said it was still the old country, which in his own neighbourhood had been swept away. Small enclosures with hedgeway timber, cottages with thatched coverings, and old-style farm houses with red-tiled roofs delighted him. To crown all, there was in the parish a fine Elizabethan mansion, the residence of Lord Walsingham, which was surrounded by fine oak trees and woods.

Fitz-Gerald exhibited in many ways his attachment to the rector and his sisters. He had known them from childhood. Their father, who for more than twenty years lived within two miles of Fitz-Gerald's cottage at Boulge, was his bosom friend, and the son whom he now went to visit had many qualities that won for him a place in

Edward Fitz-Gerald

Fitz-Gerald's affections. The Rev. George Crabbe of the third generation was of modest mien, free from self-seeking and self-assertion, warm in his friendships, securing the esteem and love of others. He possessed a cultivated taste, taking pleasure in painting and architecture, and was a student of archæology. Suffering from delicate health, he passed many winters away from home in the milder climates of Mentone and Bournemouth, and had visited Rome, Madrid, and Northern Italy. At the time of Fitz-Gerald's visit Crabbe was sixty-four years of age, and in taste, knowledge, and disposition, was as suitable a companion as could be wished for Fitz-Gerald, who showed his appreciation by making him one of his executors, bequeathing him the sum of £500 for his trouble, and leaving a legacy of £1,000 to his eldest sister.

On the morning of Wednesday, June 13th, 1883, Fitz-Gerald left Woodbridge for Merton Rectory. The journey was tedious, as the village is located in an out-of-the-way part of Norfolk. Charles Keene, who had accompanied Fitz-Gerald on one of these annual visits, said they had to change five times in getting there by rail, besides having to wait four hours at Norwich. On this last visit, however, Fitz-Gerald went by way of Bury St. Edmunds and Thetford, and his friend Crabbe met him at Watton Station, about three miles from Merton rectory. The rector's sisters were at the door to welcome him, after which he had a wash and a brush up before he sat down to tea. Then he talked of the old Abbey at Bury St. Edmunds, and the beautiful remains of its former greatness which he had just seen; charming his host by his descriptions. The heat of the day seemed to have tired him, the dust had annoyed him, and he said on his arrival that he felt 'so dirty.' Later on he was in better spirits, talked much as

Edward Fitz-Gerald

usual about old times, and walked with his friend in the grounds surrounding the house, which brought into memory scenes and persons familiar to him through his annual visits.

He had an agreeable gossip over the supper-table, but refrained from partaking of food, and about ten o'clock retired to rest. Mr. Crabbe went upstairs with him, and beyond a feeling of fatigue arising from the journey, there was nothing to cause any uneasiness on the part of his friends. Next morning, before the breakfast hour, his friend went to the chamber door to enquire how he was after the night's rest, and getting no response opened the door, went in, and found him apparently sleeping, but in reality dead. At the age of seventy-four, from the midst of his quiet and unpretentious occupations, he passed painlessly into that perfect rest that remaineth for the people of God.

It was with Fitz-Gerald as with others. He had outlived most of his contemporaries, and as life became circumscribed, interest in it diminished: memories rather than personalities had to be appealed to. Among others, Carlyle, Thackeray, Donne, Spedding had vanished, leaving Fitz-Gerald on the bank, a pathetic lonely figure, peering into futurity, it may be, conjecturing what death was like, forewarned and forearmed for the last conflict in which he would have to play his part. The end was, if not dramatic, striking alike in its suddenness and tenderness. Of his friends, Thackeray alone crossed the bar on a like peaceful ripple. That a man who had few enjoyments of domestic life, having a wife but none of the pleasures of the marriage state, having a house but not in the true sense of the word a home, and thus tasting little of the sweetness of life; that he should leave his lonely retreat to end his days under the roof of his most intimate friends; that his last hours should be with the son and the daughters of one

Edward Fitz-Gerald

who was his dearest friend; that with them he should call up old memories, and perchance open up new hopes; that, as he left them for the night the Angel of Death should be hovering over him, and that ere the break of day, light and darkness were all the same to him, for again he would know neither—all this sounds like the romance, rather than the actuality, of life; all the same Fitz-Gerald had gone to that 'bourne whence no traveller returns.' What there is of sadness in sudden death was felt in that secluded rectory house wherein an honoured guest had said his last farewell, and paid his last visit.

Save those who lay violent hands upon themselves, none can prescribe the method or means by which they shall turn their faces to the wall; but I am fain to believe that had Fitz-Gerald had the opportunity of selecting the manner of his exit, he would have preferred none to that silent, painless summons, which came in the hush of night whilst the world slumbered and slept. The meeting of Death and Fitz-Gerald was in harmony with his life. He was, so to say, lonely to the end; somewhat of a recluse in life, he was humoured in the manner of leaving it; he troubled no one, nor was he troubled on his part by the grim functions which custom and nature have set up around deathbeds. If the manner of his death was in harmony with his life, surely no more fitting spot for bidding adieu to the world could have been found than Merton rectory. 'By a divine instinct, men's minds mistrust ensuing dangers,' so it is said. Whatever thoughts led Fitz-Gerald to his friends, it was well that his eyes closed amongst those whom he had affectionately embraced from childhood, and who, apart from their own merits, were loved by him as the children of one to whom he was warmly attached. There was a keen touch of human nature about Fitz-Gerald; he loved his lost friends in their offspring.

Edward Fitz-Gerald

The following lines written by Mrs. Barbauld, and the authorship of which Wordsworth is said to have coveted, convey far better than I can express Edward Fitz-Gerald's view of life and death:—

> 'Life, I know not what thou art,
> But know that thou and I must part;
> And when or how or where we met
> I own to me is a secret yet.
> Life! we have been long together,
> Through pleasant and through cloudy weather;
> 'Tis hard to part when friends are dear;
> Perhaps 'twill cost a sigh, a tear;
> Then, steal away, give little warning;
>   Choose thine own time,
>   Say not "Good night," but in some brighter clime
>   Bid me "Good morning."'

His remains were removed to his residence 'Little Grange,' Woodbridge, and on Tuesday, June 19th, were interred in a plain earthen grave in Boulge Churchyard, surrounded by the graves of the labouring poor—a quiet resting place, shut in from the park by graceful trees, and silent but for the songs of birds and the hum of insects. He disliked ostentation, and by direction of the executors the funeral was conducted in accordance with what were known to be his wishes. The coffin, of plain oak, with brass furniture, was covered with wreaths and crosses — one of them, a beautiful wreath, being sent by Alfred Tennyson, Poet Laureate. His friend Archdeacon Groome mentioned that, not long before his decease, he expressed a wish that if any text were put upon his tombstone, it should be one which (as he said) he did not remember ever to have seen similarly used. The inscription on the granite slab which covers the grave is—' Edward Fitz-Gerald, born 31st March 1809, Died 14th June 1883. "*It is He that hath made us, and not we ourselves.*" '

Around the grave old friends, tried friends, loving friends gathered. Many who for years had been numbered among his

Edward Fitz-Gerald

dearest companions—men who had long before learnt to love the simple habits and unaffected manner of Fitz-Gerald, as much as they were proud of his great abilities as displayed in his literary work. They comprised his nephews, Mr. Walter and Mr. Edmund Kerrich, Rev. E. G. Doughty, Rev. George Crabbe, The Venerable Archdeacon Groome, Professor Cowell, Mr. Mowbray Donne, Mr. F. C. Brooke, Rev. R. C. M. Rouse, Major Rolla Rouse, Mr. Aldis Wright, Mr. W. E. Crowfoot, Mr. Richard Jones, Mr. Herman Biddell, Mr. F. Spalding, and many others. Foster in his *Life of Goldsmith*, says that at his funeral a large number of poor people came as mourners. In a similar way, folk of the same class attended at the burial of Edward Fitz-Gerald. They grieved for the loss of him who had never forgotten to be kind and charitable to them.

In the literary world, posthumous justice has not been denied to Fitz-Gerald, but the

The Life of

work of the man was very slightly valued by the public whilst he lived, and thus he was never conscious of the fame that awaited him. The English people are certainly open to reproach on this score, no matter whether the subject relates to Art or Letters. The value of Fitz-Gerald's Persian translations, was far more quickly recognised in America than in England. Fortunately those Englishmen who appreciated the power and beauty of Fitz-Gerald's work were men of influence, who were able to impregnate the thought of the age, and by this means the small band of worshippers of Omar increased year by year, and in 1892 the 'Omar Khayyám Club,' which might more appropriately be named the Edward Fitz-Gerald Club, was formed.

The year after its formation, that is, ten years after Fitz-Gerald's decease, a number of literary gentlemen from London, members of the Club, made a pilgrimage to the grave of Edward Fitz-Gerald, for the purpose of

Edward Fitz-Gerald

planting a rose tree thereon. The rose was developed from seeds taken from Omar's grave, and grafted on an English stock. To Mr. William Simpson of the *Illustrated London News*, the friends were indebted for this graceful tribute to Fitz-Gerald's memory. The planting of the tree, was performed by Mr. Curtis, head gardener at Boulge Hall, and before the ceremony was over, a shower came very appropriately, as if to bless the effort.

Mr. Simpson, when addressing the friends around the grave, explained how, accompanying the Afghan Boundary Commission from Teheran to Central Asia in 1884, the route lay near Naishápúr, the capital of Khorassan in the time of Omar, in which the poet astromoner was born, and in which he was buried. Through Fitz-Gerald's version, the Quatrains of Omar had long been highly prized by Mr. Simpson. This made him anxious to visit the grave of the poet, and on being conducted to the desolate city, he found the tomb of the old 'Tent Maker' still preserved, and his expressed wish that his grave might be where the north wind may strew roses upon it had been lovingly responded to. Mr. Edward Clodd has remarked, 'Omar Khayyám has been dead nigh eight hundred years, but his words have not passed away. Roses still scatter their petals by his resting-place.[1] And luckily it happened that Mr. Simpson was there in the autumn, when the bushes were in seed. He gathered some of the hips, and sent them to Mr. Quaritch. That gentleman forwarded them to Mr. Thistleton Dyer, the director of Kew Gardens, and under his watchful care a bush was successfully reared, but owing to climatic conditions it could only be made strong enough for planting by being grafted on a lusty English stock. When Mr. Simpson repeated his story to his old friend Edward Clodd, they agreed that the fittest

[1] Pilgrimage to Edward Fitz-Gerald's Grave.

Edward Fitz-Gerald

thing to do was to plant a cutting from this rose tree on Fitz-Gerald's grave, and into this idea Mr. Thistleton Dyer and the members of the Omar Club entered heartily. 'I understand,' said Mr. Simpson, 'by this means, the Persian rose here planted, will now bloom on English soil, a fitting emblem of the manner in which the Persian rhymes, by being grafted on to English verse, have flourished, and wafted to us the fine scent of Omar's poetic words.' He concluded by reciting an appropriate verse written for the occasion by Mr. Grant Allen, who regretted that he could not be with his friends at this meeting.

> 'Here on Fitz-Gerald's grave from Omar's tomb,
>   To lay fit tribute, pilgrim singers flock;
> Long with a double fragrance let it bloom,
>   This rose of Iran on an English Stock.'

Mr. Moncure Conway said: 'It gives me great pleasure as an American to say how dear to many of us over there is the poetry of Omar Khayyám, and how much gratitude we have always felt to Edward Fitz-Gerald for having not merely translated him, but interpreted him, so that it is almost like the reappearance of Omar Khayyám in an English heart and an English brain.' Mr. Edward Clodd, the organiser of the movement, read some dedicatory verses by Mr. Edmund Gosse, after which a few words of acknowledgment from Colonel Kerrich, a nephew, and one of Fitz-Gerald's executors, followed the attachment of a plate bearing this inscription to the grave:—

> 'This Rose-Tree raised in Kew Gardens from seed brought by William Simpson, artist traveller, from the grave of Omar Khayyám at Naish á púr, was planted by a few admirers of Edward Fitz-Gerald in the name of the Omar Khayyám Club.

'7th October 1893.'[1]

Sir William Brampton Gurdon, K.C.M.G., kindly invited the party to luncheon at

[1] Pilgrimage to Edward Fitz-Gerald's Grave.

Edward Fitz-Gerald

Grundisburgh Hall, after which some excellent quatrains, contributed by the President of the Omar Khayyám Club, Mr. Justin Huntly M'Carthy, were read, as under:—

From Naishápúr to England, from the tomb
Where Omar slumbers to the Narrow Room
That shrines Fitz-Gerald's ashes, Persia sends
Perfume and Pigment of her Rose to bloom.

Wedded with rose of England, for a sign
That English lips, transmuting the divine
High piping music of the song that ends,
As it began, with Wine, and Wine, and Wine.

Across the ages caught the words that fell
From Omar's mouth, and made them audible
To the unnumbered sitters at Life's Feast
Who wear their hearts out over Heaven and Hell.

Vex not to-day with wonder which were best,
The Student, Scholar, Singer of the West,
Or Singer, Scholar, Student of the East,
The soul of Omar burned in England's breast.

And howsoever Autumn's breezes blow
About this Rose, and Winter's fingers throw
In mockery of Oriental noons
Upon this grass the monumental snow.

The Life of

Still in our dreams the Eastern Rose survives
Lending diviner fragrance to our lives;
The World is old, cold, warned by waning moons,
But Omar's creed in English verse revives.

The fountain in the tulip-tinted dale,
The manuscript of some melodious tale
Babbling of love and lover's passion-pale,
Of Rose, of Cypress, and of Nightingale.

The cup that Saki proffers to our lips,
The cup from which the Rose-Red Mercy drips,
Bidding forget how, like a sinking sail,
Day after day into the darkness slips;

The wisdom that the Watcher of the Skies
Won from the wandering stars that soothed his eyes,
The legend writ below, around, above,
'One thing at least is certain, this Life flies';

These were the gifts of Omar—these he gave
Full handed: his Disciple sought to save
Some portion for his people, and their love
Plants Omar's Rose upon an English grave.

Mr. Edward Clodd has kindly permitted me to reprint from his privately printed *Pilgrimage*, a stanza from the poetic tribute sent by Mr Theodore Watts:—

Edward Fitz-Gerald

PRAYER TO THE WINDS.

Hear us, ye winds, North, East, and West, and South;
This granite covers him whose golden mouth
Made wiser ev'n the word of Wisdom's King;
Blow softly o'er the grave of Omar's herald
Till roses rich of Omar's dust shall spring
From richer dust of Suffolk's rare Fitz-Gerald.

APPENDIX

COPY OF THE WILL OF EDWARD FITZ-GERALD

THIS is the Last Will and Testament of me, EDWARD FITZ-GERALD, of Woodbridge, in the County of Suffolk, Esquire, made this third day of April one thousand eight hundred and eighty-three. I appoint my nephew Lieutenant-Colonel Edmund Kerrich and my friends the Reverend George Crabbe of Merton Watton in the County of Norfolk, Clerk, and the Reverend Ernest George Doughty of Martlesham in the County of Suffolk, Clerk, Executors of this my Will, and Trustees for the purposes hereinafter mentioned: I direct that all my just debts and my funeral and testamentary expenses may be paid as soon as conveniently can be after my decease, and that my funeral may be conducted in a simple and inexpensive manner; and I direct my said executors to reward handsomely at their discretion all persons who may be in my service at the time of my decease, or who may have attended or waited upon me during my last illness, each according to desert (except those especially provided for by this my Will,

Will of Edward Fitz-Gerald

and those, if any, whom I may specially reward or provide for by any Codicil or Codicils to this my Will): I give, devise, and bequeath all and every the freehold and leasehold messuages, lands, tenements, hereditaments, and premises whereof or whereto I or any person or persons in trust for me am, are, or is seized or entitled, or which I have power to give or dispose of by this my Will, whether in possession, reversion, remainder, or expectancy, with the appurtenances (save and except such as are vested in me in trust or by way of mortgage), unto and to the use of the said Edmund Kerrich, George Crabbe, and Ernest George Doughty, their heirs, executors, administrators, and assigns according to the nature of the said estates respectively upon trust: and I do authorise, empower, and direct my said trustees, or the trustees or trustee for the time being, under this my will, with all convenient speed after my decease, to make, sale, and dispose of my said freehold and leasehold estates; and I also authorise, empower, and direct my trustees or trustee for the time being to make, sale, and dispose of all the copyhold or customary messuages, lands, tenements, and hereditaments of or to which I or any person or persons in trust for me may be seized or entitled at the time of my decease, and I direct that such hereditaments (freehold, leasehold, and copyhold) may be sold either together or in parcels, and by public auction or private contract, for the most money and best prices that can be reasonably obtained

Appendix

for the same, and with liberty to buy in and resell the same or any part or parts thereof at discretion, and I declare that the net proceeds of sale of my said real and leasehold estates, after paying the expenses of and attending such sale, shall sink into and form part of my personal estate; I give to each of them, the said George Crabbe and Ernest George Doughty, the sum of five hundred pounds for his care and trouble in the execution of the trusts of this my Will; I give to Margaret, Honoria, and Mary Frances, three of the daughters of my Uncle Peter Purcell, now or late of Halverstown, County Kildare, Ireland, the sum of five hundred pounds each; and I also give to Eva Purcell, a grand-daughter of my said Uncle Peter Purcell, the sum of five hundred pounds; I give to William Biddell, now of Lavenham Hall, in the County of Suffolk, Esquire, M.P., and the Reverend Francis Bathurst, Vicar of Diddington, Huntingdonshire, the sum of one thousand pounds sterling, upon trust, to invest the same in their names in Government Funds or on Mortgage securities at interest, or in Bank Stock or Railway Debentures (with power at discretion to vary the securities for others of a like nature), and upon further trust that they or the survivor of them or his executors or administrators, or their or his assigns, shall pay the annual dividends, interest, and proceeds thereof, when and as the same shall be received, to and between Edith Airy, Sybel Airy, Mabel Airy, and Beatrice Airy, four of the daughters

Will of Edward Fitz-Gerald

of the Reverend William Airy of Keysoe in the County of Bedford, in equal shares, with benefit of survivorship between them; and upon the death of the last survivor of them I direct that the whole of the principal of the said trust fund shall be divided equally between and amongst the issue (if any) of such of them as shall die leaving lawful issue, share and share alike, *per capita*; and if all of them, the said four daughters, shall die without leaving lawful issue, then I direct that the whole of the said trust fund shall be paid to the last surviving daughter, her executors, administrators, or assigns, for her or their own absolute use and benefit, to whom I give and bequeath the same accordingly: I give the sum of one thousand pounds equally between all the daughters of Frederick Tennyson of Saint Heliers, in the Island of Jersey, Esquire, to be paid to them as soon as conveniently can be after the decease of the survivor of myself and my wife Lucy Fitz-Gerald, with benefit of survivorship between them in case of the death of any of them in the lifetime of myself or my said wife without leaving lawful issue; but if any of them shall be then dead leaving lawful issue, each issue shall take the share which their, his, or her deceased mother would have been entitled to if living, equally if more than one, and if but one the whole to such one; I give to Caroline Matilda Crabbe, a daughter of the late Reverend George Crabbe of Bredfield in the County of Suffolk, Clerk, the sum of one thousand pounds, and if

Appendix

she should die in my lifetime I give the said sum of one thousand pounds to her sister Mary Crabbe: I give to Arthur Charlesworth, third son of Edward Charlesworth, formerly of York, the sum of one hundred pounds; I give to Horace Basham of Aldeburgh-on-Sea, in the County of Suffolk, the sum of one hundred pounds; I give the sum of one hundred pounds to Laura, Anna, Harriet, and Kate (or Catharine), four of the daughters of the late Thomas Churchyard of Woodbridge, Solicitor, to be equally divided between them, with benefit of survivorship in case of the death of any or either of them in my lifetime; I give to Anne, the wife of Mr. Richmond Ritchie (the eldest daughter of the late William Makepeace Thackeray), the sum of five hundred pounds; I give to Miss Marietta Nursey, daughter of the late Mr. Perry Nursey of Little Bealings in the said County of Suffolk, an annuity or clear yearly sum of thirty pounds; and I give to John Howe and Mary Anne, his wife, now in my service, an annuity or clear yearly sum of seventy pounds for their joint lives and the life of the longer liver of them, and at the decease of the longer liver of them I give the sum of one hundred pounds to be equally divided between their two sons, John Howe and George Howe; I give to Emilius Cologan of Number 13 Percy Street, Rathbone Place, London, an annuity or clear yearly sum of fifteen pounds for his life; and I charge the said several annuities of thirty pounds, seventy pounds,

Will of Edward Fitz-Gerald

and fifteen pounds on my residuary personal estate and proceeds hereinafter directed to be invested, and direct the payment thereof respectively quarterly, on the sixth day of January, the sixth day of April, and the sixth day of July, and the eleventh day of October, with a proportionate part thereof to the decease of the respective annuitants, a proportionate part of the first quarterly payment from the day of my decease to be paid on such of the said days as shall happen next after my decease: And I declare that the trusts hereinafter contained for disposition of such residue shall be subject to such annuities and the legacy or succession duties thereon; and I declare that the said respective annuitants shall not be entitled to elect to receive the price or value of their respective annuities in lieu of such annuities; and I also declare that if the said respective annuitants shall at any time sell, assign, alien, encumber, or transfer, or in anywise dispose of or anticipate their respective annuities, or any part thereof respectively, then and in such cases respectively, and immediately thereupon, the annuity so dealt with shall sink into and become part of the residue of my personal estate: I give to the treasurer for the time being of the East Suffolk Hospital at Ipswich the sum of one hundred pounds, to be applied to the uses of that Institution, and to be paid out of my pure personality within one year from my decease, and the receipt of such treasurer for the time being of the said Institution shall be a sufficient

Appendix

discharge to my executors; I give to my niece Eleanor Frances Kerrich, the eldest daughter of the late John Kerrich of Geldeston, Norfolk, the sum of six hundred pounds (in addition to her share as a residuary legatee under this my Will), and I give or forgive to the said Edmund Kerrich, and to any other of the legatees under this my Will who now is, or are, or may be, at the time of my decease, indebted to me all debts and monies that may be owing by him or them respectively; I give my painting, the Titian landscape of Abraham and Isaac, which usually hangs opposite the fireplace in my dining-room, to the Fitz-William Museum in Cambridge; I give my painting, the portrait of Raphael Mengs, which usually hangs over the bureau by the French window in my sitting-room, to Mr. John Loder of Woodbridge, stationer; I give all such articles, whether furniture, books, pictures, or other things that may be specially marked, or a list whereof may be left by me as intended for any of my friends, to the person or persons to be so designated by me; I direct that all legacies and annuities given by this my Will shall be paid or delivered to the respective legatees, or annuitants, free of legacy duty; and as to all the residue and remainder of my real and personal estate and effects whatsoever and wheresoever, I give the same to my executors, the said Edmund Kerrich, George Crabbe, and Ernest George Doughty, their heirs, executors, administrators, and assigns; Upon trust (subject to the carrying out of the

Will of Edward Fitz-Gerald

desire and request contained in my Will as to the delivery of pictures, books, or other articles to my friends) that they, the said Edmund Kerrich, George Crabbe, and Ernest George Doughty, or the survivor of them, his executors or administrators, shall and do as soon as conveniently can be after my decease convert into money in such manner as they or he may think proper (but subject to the direction and authority hereinafter contained as to continuing and appropriating investments existing at my decease) such part or parts of the said residue and remainder as shall not consist of money or securities for money, and invest the money to arise therefrom, and all ready money in their or his names or name in Government funds, or on Mortgage securities at interest, or in Bank Stock or Railway Debentures (with power at discretion to vary the investments or securities for others of a like nature), and shall and do stand possessed of and interested in such stocks, funds, and securities ; Upon trust to pay and divide the dividends, interest, and annual produce thereof in equal shares unto, between, and amongst my nephews and nieces ten of the children (eight daughters and two sons) of the late John Kerrich of Geldeston Hall, in the County of Norfolk, Esquire, and Eleanor his wife, namely, Eleanor Frances, Elizabeth, Amelia Jane, Mary, Andalusia, Anna Maria Theresa, Adeline Walker, Eleanor, Edmund and John, or such of them as may be living at the time of my decease, and the issue (per stirpes) of such of them as may be then

Appendix

dead leaving lawful issue, the share of each niece to be for her separate use, independent of any husband, and so that she shall not have power to deprive herself of the benefit thereof by sale, mortgage, charge, or otherwise by way of anticipation, and at the expiration of ten years from my decease (subject nevertheless, as hereinafter mentioned, with respect to the share of my niece the wife of   Funajoli), do and shall pay, transfer, and divide the said trust funds unto, between, and amongst all and every my said nephews and nieces hereinbefore named (the children of the said John and Eleanor Kerrich) then living, and the issue of any of them who may be then dead leaving lawful issue, such issue taking equally, if more than one, the share of their, his, or her parent or respective parents, and I direct that the share of any minor shall and may be paid to either of the parents (at the discretion of my said trustees), or to the Guardian of such minor whose receipt shall be a good discharge for the same, and shall exonerate my said trustees from all liability in respect thereof; Provided nevertheless, and I hereby direct that the share of my said niece Mary Funajoli as one of my residuary legatees shall not be paid to her, but shall be held by the said Edmund Kerrich and invested upon any of the securities hereinbefore mentioned, and the dividend, interest, and produce thereof shall be paid to her for her life, free from the control, debts, or engagements of her present or any future husband; and from and

Will of Edward Fitz-Gerald

after decease I direct that the said share and the stocks, funds, and securities upon which the same may be invested shall be held by the said Edmund Kerrich, his executors, or administrators upon trust for such of the children of her my said niece Mary Funajoli at such ages or times and in such manner in all respects as she shall by her will, or any writing in the nature of a will, to be made by her either when sole or under coverture, appoint, and in default of such appointment, then upon trust to pay and divide the same equally between all the children of her my said niece living at her decease, and the issue (per stirpes) of such of them as may be then dead leaving lawful issue, to whom I give the same accordingly (to be a vested interest at their respective ages of twenty-one years); I direct that my said executors or executor for the time being may (subject to the direction and authority hereinafter contained as to continuing and appropriating existing securities) from time to time sell and dispose of securities and investments, whether existing at my decease or made by them or him, and invest the proceeds in any of the stocks, funds, and securities hereinbefore specified, and may in their or his discretion from time to time vary such investments for any other of a like nature; I empower my trustees or trustee for the time being in their or his discretion to advance and apply any part not exceeding one-half of the capital to which under any of the bequests or dispositions contained in this my Will any

Appendix

minor may be entitled or presumptively entitled in or towards the preferment or advancement in the world of such minor; I direct that my executors or executor shall provide for payment of such legacies as may under this my Will or any Codicil or Codicils which I may hereafter make, be payable at my decease, and the duty thereon, by calling in any mortgage or mortgages that may be due to my estate, or by selling out such stock or realising such investment or investments as can be sold out or realised with the least loss of the capital originally invested; and it is my wish that no trustees or trustee under this my Will or any Codicil or Codicils which I may hereafter make, shall sell out from any investment reasonably considered a safe investment made by me or by themselves or himself which may have fallen in value since the time of investment (provided dividends thereon are regularly paid) if such a course can possibly be avoided; and I also direct that my executors or executor for the time being may appropriate any investment existing at my decease, and which cannot be then sold out except at a loss, as part of the trust funds hereinbefore directed to be invested for the benefit of the Kerrich family at the values current at the time of such appropriation, my desire being that no sale should be effected at a loss if it can possibly be avoided, and that my executors or executor for the time being shall have sole and absolute discretion and authority as to all such appropriations, and I desire and request my said

Will of Edward Fitz-Gerald

nephews and nieces and their issue to invest, or cause to be invested, their respective legacies and shares or portions, when paid to them, in some publicly guaranteed safe investment, British or Foreign, and not in any private speculation whatever, or by whomsoever solicited, and I rely on their obeying this my solemn injunction; I devise all real estate vested in me as a trustee or mortgagee unto my said trustees the said Edmund Kerrich, George Crabbe, and Ernest George Doughty, their heirs and assigns, upon the trusts, and subject to the equities affecting the same respectively; I direct that all legacies and monies to be paid to females by virtue of this my Will shall be for their own respective sole use and benefit, and their respective receipts alone shall, notwithstanding their coverture, be good discharges for the same; I declare that if the trustees respectively hereby constituted, or any or either of them, or any trustee or trustees to be appointed as hereinafter provided, shall die, or be about to reside abroad, or desire to be discharged, or become bankrupt or insolvent, or refuse or become incapable to act in the execution of the aforesaid trusts, or any of them, before the same trusts shall be fully executed and performed, then and in every such case it shall be lawful for the surviving or continuing trustee (if any) for the time being (and for this purpose a retiring trustee, if willing to act in the execution of this present power, shall be deemed a continuing trustee), or if there shall be no sur-

Appendix

viving or continuing trustee, then for the executors or administrators of the last surviving trustee to nominate, substitute, and appoint any other person or persons to be a trustee or trustees in the place or stead of the trustee or trustees so dying, or being about to reside abroad, or desiring to be discharged, or becoming bankrupt or insolvent, or refusing or becoming incapable to act as aforesaid, and upon every such nomination and appointment as aforesaid all the trust estate, monies, stocks, funds, and securities for the time being, subject to the trusts of this my Will respectively, shall with all convenient speed be conveyed, assigned, or otherwise assured, so that the same may become legally and effectually vested in such new trustee or trustees jointly with the surviving or continuing trustee or trustees (if any), or in such new trustee or trustees solely as the case may require, upon and for the several trusts, intents, and purposes, and with, under, and subject to the several powers, provisoes, and agreements hereinbefore expressed, declared, and contained of and concerning the same respectively, or such and so many of the same trusts, intents and purposes, powers, provisoes, and agreements as shall be then subsisting, undetermined, or capable of taking effect; and every new trustee as well before as after the said trust property shall have been so vested in him shall and may have and exercise all the same powers, authorities, and directions, as if he had been hereby originally nominated and

Will of Edward Fitz-Gerald

appointed a trustee; Lastly, I revoke all former Wills and Testamentary Dispositions by me made, and do declare this to be my last Will and Testament, IN WITNESS WHEREOF I have to this my last Will and Testament contained in nine sheets of paper set my hand the day and year first above written.

Signed by the said EDWARD FITZ-GERALD, the Testator, as his last Will and Testament, in the presence of us present at the same time, who in his sight and presence, and in the presence of each other, subscribe our names as witnesses.

EDWARD FITZ-GERALD.

F. W. W. Gross, Solicitor, Woodbridge.
John Brightwell, Woodbridge.

Proved at Ipswich the 24th day of July 1883 by the oaths of Edmund Kerrich, the nephew; the Reverend George Crabbe, Clerk, and the Reverend Ernest George Doughty, Clerk, the executors, to whom admon was granted.

G. W. H.

LETTER FROM MRS. EDWARD FITZ-GERALD.

3 CHICHESTER PLACE,
BRIGHTON, *June* 14*th*, 1865.

SIR,—I was from home the day your letter reached Brighton, which must be my excuse for having delayed my answer for a day or two. I like to hear of your proposed volume, as I think there are some poems, and those not very widely known perhaps, of which Suffolk may well be proud. Are poems which have been published in a pocket-book public property? If they are, there are some of Mrs. Fulcher's published in her husband's Sudbury pocket-book which are *very* beautiful, but you probably know them. You will also find several poems in that pocket-book by Miss Charlesworth (now Mrs. Edward Cowell); they are specified as 'by the Author of *Historical Reveries*'; but as I believe Mrs. Cowell is now in England with her husband, it might be better to ask her about it. I know but little of Mr. Mitford's poetry, but I remember years ago he used to contribute to Raw's *Pocket-Book*; in that P.-B. for 1832 there are several poems by Mr. Mitford, one especially a beautiful sonnet to Charles Lamb (Elia) on his poem called 'Leisure.' But probably at Ipswich you can see the old Pocket-Books, and gather from them many that I have forgotten. I remember a fine poem of his written at the time of the Thurtell and Weir murder, beginning, 'The maple's head is

Letter from Mrs. Fitz-Gerald

glowing red, and red is the glow of the western sky,' which I think appeared in Raw's *Pocket-Book*.

I know no poems of Miss Catherine Strickland; her sister Agnes used to write in Pawsey's *Pocket-Book*. Do you know a lovely poem of the late Mrs. Biddell of Playford?—she was the sister of Mr. James and Robert Ransome. The lines were written on the 'Old Foundry,' when it gave place many years since to a new one, and begins:—

> 'The furnace fires are out, ye lathes are still,
>   The engine puffs its fiery breath no more;
> No longer now is heard the groaning mill,
>   No busy feet are trampling on ye floor.'

Altogether there are twelve stanzas of great beauty and tenderness. I have them in MS.; they were sent by her to my dear father; but whether they were ever printed in Pawsey's P.-B. or elsewhere I know not. Her lines written in the park of Christchurch, Ipswich, at page 228 of the *Old Suffolk Garland*, are probably familiar to you.

As to my own verses, you must not think me insensible to your implied compliment in proposing to reprint anything of mine in your present *Miscellany*; but I never wrote anything worthy of the name of poetry, and I shall esteem it a great kindness if you will altogether leave me out. I think the verses you mention on the death of Priscilla Wakefield cannot be mine, for I have not the slightest recollection of having written them.

I wish I could have been more useful to you. —Believe me, dear sir, yours truly,

LUCY FITZ-GERALD.

CERTIFICATE OF MARRIAGE

1856

Marriage solemnised in the Parish Church, in the Parish of All Saints', in the County of Sussex.

Columns	1	2	3	4	5	6	7	8
No.	When Married.	Name and Surname.	Age.	Condition.	Rank or Profession.	Residence at the time of Marriage.	Father's Name and Surname.	Rank or Profession of Father.
34	Nov. 4, 1856.	Edward Fitzgerald,	full,	Bachelor,	Gentleman,	Woodbridge, Suffolk,	John FitzGerald,	Gentleman.
		Lucy Barton,	full,	Spinster,	..	Extra Parochial District of St. John's, Chichester,	Bernard Barton,	Gentleman.

Married in the Parish Church, according to the Rites and Ceremonies of the Church of England and Ireland, by T. R. DRAKE, *Rector*.

This Marriage was solemnised between us, { EDWARD FITZ-GERALD, LUCY BARTON, } in the Presence of us, { Josephine C. Rickman, Emily Barton, Anne Barton, Elizabeth Barton, Joseph Barton, Gerald Barton.

The above is a true Copy of the Marriage Register of the Parish aforesaid, extracted this thirteenth day of January, in the year of our Lord one thousand eight hundred and ninety-seven,
By me F. T. BIRKETT,
Rector of All Saints', Chichester.

BIBLIOGRAPHY

of the versions and editions of the *Rubáiyát* of Omar Khayyám, by Edward Fitz-Gerald and others, which have been published in England, the United States, and on the Continent. Arranged according to date of publication.

1. *Rubáiyát* of Omar Khayyám, the astronomer-poet of Persia. Translated into English verse. London: Bernard Quaritch, 1859. Small 4to, brown paper wrappers. Pp. xiii + 21.
    This edition, the first of Fitz-Gerald's, not finding buyers, was ultimately sold off by Mr. Quaritch at a penny a copy. During the last few years the demand for it has been keen; and in February 1898 a copy in the original brown paper wrapper was, after a smart competition in Sotheby's rooms, knocked down for £21.
2. *Rubáiyát* of Omar Khayyám, the astronomer-poet of Persia, rendered into Eng-

Bibliography

lish verse. Second edition. London: Bernard Quaritch, Piccadilly, 1868. Small 4to, wrappers. Pp. xviii + 30.

In this edition there are alterations and additions.

3. *Rubáiyát* of Omar Khayyám, the astronomer-poet of Persia, rendered into English verse. London: Bernard Quaritch, Piccadilly, 1872. Quarto, half-Roxburghe. Pp. xxiv + 36.

In this edition the quatrains are considerably increased.

Neither of the above-named editions have the name of the translator. They were issued anonymously, and twelve years elapsed before even Thomas Carlyle discovered that his friend, Edward Fitz-Gerald, was the translator.

4. *Rubáiyát* of Omar Khayyám, the astronomer-poet of Persia, rendered into English verse. Boston: James R. Osgood & Company, 1878. Square 16mo. Pp. 78. Verses blank; red line ($1.00).

This is the first American edition.

5. *Rubáiyát* of Omar Khayyám and the Sálámin and Absál of Jami, rendered into English verse. Bernard Quaritch: Piccadilly, London, 1879. Fcap. 4to, half-Roxburghe. Pp. xvi + 112.

6. The Quilter edition. Omar Khayyám,

Bibliography

the *Rubáiyát*, translated into English verse. Royal 4to, title printed on the covers. London: John Campbell, jun., 1883.

7. The Vedder Illustrated edition. *Rubáiyát* of Omar Khayyám, with ornamental title-page, and 56 full-page drawings, by Elihu Vedder. Folio, cloth, gilt top. Boston, 1884 ($100.00 net).

8. The Grolier edition. *Rubáiyát* of Omar Khayyám, the astronomer-poet of Persia, rendered into English verse by Edward Fitz-Gerald. The Grolier Club of New York, 1885. Medium octavo, printed from old-style types. Covers of Japan paper beautifully ornamented from an Oriental design.

9. Whinfield, E. H. The Quatrains of Omar Khayyám, translated into English verse. 253 quatrains, octavo. Pp. viii+91. London, 1882.

10. The Phototype edition. This is an edition of the Vedder Illustrated, reduced in size, with the engravings phototyped. Quarto, cloth, gilt top. Boston, 1886 ($12.50).

11. The Memorial edition. Works of Edward Fitz-Gerald, translator of Omar Khayyám, reprinted from the original impressions, with some corrections derived from his own annotated copies.

Bibliography

New York and Boston: Houghton, Mifflin & Co. London: Bernard Quaritch, 1887. 2 vols. octavo ($10.00).

A few large-paper copies, royal octavo, were issued at $25.00.

12. The Comparative edition. *Rubáiyát* of Omar Khayyám, in English verse, by Edward Fitz-Gerald. The text of the fourth edition, followed by that of the first, with Notes showing the extent of his indebtedness to the Persian original, and Biographical Preface. 12mo, half-vellum. Boston, 1888 ($1.50).

13. Garner, John Leslie. The Strophes of Omar Khayyám, translated from the Persian with Introduction and Notes. 142 quatrains. Square 12mo. Pp. xii + 76. Milwaukee, 1888.

A second edition of this book, printed on one side of leaf only, was issued in Philadelphia in 1898. It contains 154 quatrains.

14. Letters and Literary Remains of Edward Fitz-Gerald. Edited by William Aldis Wright. In three volumes. London: Macmillan & Co., and New York. Crown 8vo, 1889.

15. *Rubáiyát* of Omar Khayyám. Prose version by Justin Huntly M'Carthy. Fcap. 8vo, bds. Pp. lxii + clvi. Lon-

Bibliography

don, 1889. 550 copies on small paper and 60 copies on large paper were issued, printed in capital letters throughout.

An edition of this prose version was published in America in 1896.

16. *Rubáiyát* of Omar Khayyám, the astronomer-poet of Persia, rendered into English verse. London: Macmillan & Co., and New York, 1890. Crown 8vo. Pp. iv + 112.

    This is a reprint of the *Rubáiyát* by itself, from the 'Letters and Literary Remains.'

17. Pamphlet edition of *Rubáiyát* of Omar Khayyám. 12mo, green paper wrapper. Pp. 48. San Francisco, 1891 (20 cents).

18. The Old World edition. *Rubáiyát* of Omar Khayyám. Narrow fcap. 8vo, vellum boards, uncut. Containing parallel texts of the first and fourth editions, a list of the variations between the second, third, and fourth editions, quatrains printed in the second edition only, and biographies of Edward Fitz-Gerald and of Omar Khayyám, 1895. Mr. Mosher, Portland, Maine.

    Five editions of this book have been issued, each consisting of 925 copies.

Bibliography

19. Selections from the *Rubáiyát.* Octavo. Pp. 21. Boston, December 1893. Privately printed by John L. Stoddard.
20. The Multi-Variorum edition. *Rubáiyát* of Omar Khayyám. English, French, and German translations. Comparatively arranged in accordance with the text of Edward Fitz-Gerald's version, with Notes, Biographies, and Bibliographies. Edited by Nathan Haskell Dole. 2 vols. 12mo. Boston, 1896.

    There was a second edition of this book, with additions, in 1898.
21. *Rubáiyát* of Omar Khayyám of Naishápúr, the astronomer-poet of Persia, rendered into English verse. C. H. St. John Hornby, Ashendene Press, 1896. Small 4to. Pp. xl+48.
22. *Rubáiyát* of Omar Khayyám. A paraphrase from several literal translations by Richard Le Gallienne. Narrow 8vo. Pp. xvi+88. London, 1897.

    In the same year an edition was published in New York.
23. The Quatrains of Omar Khayyám, the astronomer-poet of Persia, now first completely done into English verse in the original forms, by John Payne. In all about 840 quatrains. Octavo, vellum, gilt top. The Villon Society, London, 1898.

Bibliography

24. The *Rubáiyát* of Omar Khayyám, being a facsimile of the manuscript in the Bodleian Library at Oxford, with a transcript into modern characters. Translated, with an Introduction and Notes, and a Bibliography, by Edward Heron-Allen. London: H. S. Nichols, L.T.D., 1898. Royal octavo, white leather. Pp. xiii + 287.

    A second edition of this book was issued in 1899. London: Bernard Quaritch. 7s. 6d.

25. *Rubáiyát* of Omar Khayyám, the astronomer-poet of Persia, rendered into English verse. Golden Treasury edition, 1899. Pott 8vo, 2s. 6d. net. Macmillan & Co., London.

    This edition is Fitz-Gerald's fourth, with all the variations between the second, third, and fourth editions, and a list of the stanzas which appear in second edition only.

    The following editions have no date.

26. The Crowell edition. *Rubáiyát* of Omar Khayyám, and the Salámán and Absál of Jami, rendered into English verse, by Edward Fitz-Gerald. Square 12mo. Pp. 288. New York and Boston.

27. Pamphlet edition. *Rubáiyát* of Omar Khayyám. Square 12mo, grey wrapper. Pp. 60. San Francisco (25 cents).

Bibliography

28. *Rubáiyát* of Omar Khayyám. Square 12mo, bds. Pp. 64. Published for Will Bradley by R. H. Russell, New York.

For many facts in this Bibliography I am indebted to a List issued by Mr. Mosher, Portland, Maine, who has published a larger number of Fitz-Gerald's translations than any other publisher in the United States.

BIBLIOGRAPHY

of Articles in Reviews and Magazines relating to Fitz-Gerald and Omar.

Atlantic Monthly, April 1878, 'A Persian Poet.' Thos. B. Aldrich.
Academy, Sept. 20, 1879, Fitz-Gerald's fourth edition reviewed.
Academy, Nov. 30, 1895, 'Letters of Edward Fitz-Gerald to Fanny Kemble.' R. C. Browne.
Academy, Aug. 3 1889, 'Literary Remains of Edward Fitz-Gerald.' Edward Dowden.
Athenæum, July 13, 1889, 'Literary Remains of Edward Fitz-Gerald.'
Blackwood's Magazine, Nov. 1889, 'Edward Fitz-Gerald.' F. H. Groome.
Calcutta Review, 1895, article by H. G. Keene.
Century Magazine, Nov. 1884, ' Omar.'
Cornhill Magazine, Dec. 1890, 'Omar's *Rubáiyát*.'
Contemporary Review, March 1876, 'The *Rubáiyát* of Omar.' Shultz Wilson.

Bibliography

Daily Telegraph, Aug. 15, 1879, Fitz-Gerald's fourth edition reviewed.
Dial, Nov. 1889, 'The Translator of Omar Khayyám.' Melville B. Anderson.
Dial, Oct. 1895, 'More Fitz-Gerald Letters.' E. G. J.
Edinburgh Review, Oct. 1894, 'Letters of Edward Fitz-Gerald.'
English Illustrated Magazine, Feb. 1894, 'Fitz-Gerald.' Edward Clodd.
Fortnightly Review, July 1889, 'Edward Fitz-Gerald.' Edmund Gosse.
Fortnightly Review, Dec. 1896, 'Omar.' J. A. Murray.
Fraser's Magazine, June 1870, 'Account of Omar.'
Fraser's Magazine, May 1879, 'The True Omar Khayyám.' Mrs. Cadell.
Leisure Hour, Jan. 1895, 'Edward Fitz-Gerald.' John Dennis.
Littell's Living Age, 29th March 1890, 'Edward Fitz-Gerald.'
London Quarterly Review, July 1895, 'Edward Fitz-Gerald.'
Macmillan's Magazine, Nov. 1887, 'Omar Khayyám.' H. G. Keene.
Magazine of Art, May, 'Edward Fitz-Gerald.' Sidney Colvin.
National Review, Dec. 1890, 'Omar of Naishápúr.' C. J. Pickering.
New Englander, Nov. 1888, 'Schopenhauer

Bibliography

and Omar Khayyám.' Wm. Lyon Phelps.

New Englander, Jan. and Feb. 1890, 'A Review of the Works of an English Man of Letters, Edward Fitz-Gerald.' Thos. Rutherford Bacon.

North American Review, Oct. 1869, review of Nicolas' edition of Omar.'

New York Evening Post, April 21, 1883, 'Whinfield's 1882 Version of the Quatrains of Omar Khayyám.'

Old and New (Boston, U.S.A.), May 1872, 'Poems of Omar.' Rev. J. W. Chadwick.

Pall Mall Gazette, Feb. 16, 1898, review of Heron-Allen's Edition of Fitz-Gerald's Omar.

Punch, Aug. 17, 1895, 'Five Mock *Rubáiyát*, entitled "A Query by Omar Khayyám."'

Quarterly Review, July 1896, 'Letters of Edward Fitz-Gerald.'

Scotsman, Sept. 12, 1879, Fitz-Gerald's fourth edition reviewed.

Saturday Review, Jan. 16, 1886, J. H. M'Carthy on 'Fitz-Gerald's Omar.'

Saturday Review, July 20, 1889, 'The *Rubáiyát* of Omar Khayyám.'

Saturday Review, Aug. 10, 1895, 'Past Days in East Anglia.'

Spectator, Aug. 17, 1889, 'Edward Fitz-Gerald,'

Bibliography

Spectator, Aug. 17, 1889, 'Mr. M'Carthy's Omar Khayyám.'

The Nation, Oct. 26, 1893, 'The Omar Cult in England.' Dr. M. D. Conway.

The Nation, Oct. 24, 1895, 'Fitz-Gerald and Fanny Kemble.'

Westminster Gazette, Feb. 22, 1898, J. H. M'Carthy on Heron-Allen's edition of Fitz-Gerald's Omar.

Westminster Review, March 1896, 'Edward Fitz-Gerald.' Maurice Todhunter.

For some of the references in the above list I am indebted to Mr. Edward Heron-Allen's volume on the *Rubáiyát*.

INDEX

AIRY, Rev. William—
    Legacies to his daughters, 326.
    Lifelong friend of Fitz-Gerald, 10.
Allen, Rev. John—
    Appointed Mathematical Lecturer, Examining Chaplain, and Archdeacon of Salop, 72.
    College friend of Fitz-Gerald, 13.
    Visit of Fitz-Gerald to, 218.

BARTON, Bernard, facts about, 60.
Barton, Lucy, her marriage to Fitz-Gerald, 243.
Bibliography—
    Of articles in reviews and magazines relating to Fitz-Gerald, 349.
    Of the works of Omar Khayyám, 341.
Books by Fitz-Gerald—
    Euphranor, 124.
    Polonius, 127.
    Sea Words and Phrases along the Suffolk Coast, 129.

Index

Borrow, George, a visitor to Fitz-Gerald, 235.
'Bredfield Hall,' poem by Fitz-Gerald, 120.
Brooke, Captain, as a lover of books, 208.
Buller, Charles, and others, whose friendship with Fitz-Gerald was formed at Cambridge, 18.

CALDERON'S *Six Dramas*, translated by Fitz-Gerald, 142.
Cambridge tutors, Fitz-Gerald's, 12.
Carlyle, Thomas—
    Friendship of, with Fitz-Gerald, 75.
    Letters of, to Fitz-Gerald, 228.
    Visit of, to Fitz-Gerald at Woodbridge, 223.
Cowell, Professor, Fitz-Gerald's guide in Spanish and Persian literature, 141-146.
Crabbe, Rev. George—
    Death of, 55.
    Friendship of, with Fitz-Gerald, 52.

FAWCETT, Mrs. Henry, letter from, 296.
—— Professor Henry, acquaintance of, with Fitz-Gerald, 294.
Fitz-Gerald, Edward—
    Anecdotes of, 34.
    As a host, 58.
    As a vegetarian, 41.
    At the Lakes with Tennyson, 26.
    Birth of, at Bredfield Hall, 3.

Index

Fitz-Gerald, Edward, *continued*—
    Burial of, 313.
    Childhood of, 5.
    Cottage home at Boulge, 48.
    Death of, 309.
    Description of, 83.
    Disregard of, for wealth, 106.
    Dunwich, the ruined city; meets Edwin Edwards and Charles Keene there, 286-288.
    Facts about his marriage, 246.
    Fame of, rests on his Persian translations, 185.
    Friendship of, with—
        Carlyle, 75.
        Milnes, Monckton, 252.
        Tennyson, 66.
        Thackeray, 220.
    Generosity of, 103.
    In rooms in London, 22.
    Last days of, 301.
    Letters of, to Lord Houghton, 254.
    Library of, 187.
    Life of, at Cambridge, 14.
    Literary work of, 112.
    Marriage of, 237.
    Merton Rectory, 5.
        Last visit of, to, 308.
        Sudden death of, at, 309.
    Mother of, the, 5.
    Movements of, from place to place, 32.

Index

Fitz-Gerald, Edward, *continued*—
    Persian studies of, 146.
    Personal characteristics of, 83.
    Sent to Grammar-School at Bury St. Edmunds, 8.
    Separation of, from his wife, 248.
    Settling down in a home of his own, 45.
    Social evenings held by, 56.
    Spanish literature studied by, 141.
    Stay of, at Southampton, 20.
    Visit of friends to, 268.
        of, to France when nine years old, 7.
        of, to Ireland, 78.
        of, to Kenilworth, 69.
        of, on leaving college, 18.
    Warm friendships of, 62.
    Will of, 324.
—— Mrs. Edward, letter from, 338.
—— Peter, story of, 10.

GROOME, Archdeacon, friendship of, with Fitz-Gerald, 59.

HAY, Colonel John, address of, to the Omar Khayyám Club, 176.
Houghton, Lord, friendship of, with Fitz-Gerald, 252.

KEENE, Charles, acquaintance of, with Fitz-Gerald, 288.

Index

Kemble, Fanny, her friendship with Fitz-Gerald, 277.
—— Mrs. Charles, friendship of Fitz-Gerald's mother with, 7.

LAURENCE, Samuel, friendship of, with Fitz-Gerald, 36.
Letters of Fitz-Gerald, their beauty and purity, 137.
Little Grange, description of, 261.

MARRIAGE—
    Of Fitz-Gerald with Lucy Barton, 237.
    Register, official copy of the, 353.
M'Carthy, Justin Huntly, poem to Fitz-Gerald by, 321.

OMAR KHAYYÁM—
    Facts about, 150.
    Works of, translated by Fitz-Gerald, 147.

PERSIAN studies of Fitz-Gerald, 146.
Pilgrimage to Fitz-Gerald's grave, 316.
Poems by Fitz-Gerald—
    'Bredfield Hall,' 120.
    'The Meadows in Spring,' 115.

READ, Mr. James, a famous bookseller at Ipswich, 203.

Index

Sea Words and Phrases along the Suffolk Coast, 129.
Spanish literature first studied by Fitz-Gerald, 141.
Spedding family, the, 27.
Spedding, James—
    Death of, 293.
    His friendship with Fitz-Gerald formed at school, 10.
    Visit of Fitz-Gerald to, 26.

TENNYSON, Alfred, Lord—
    At Woodbridge with Fitz-Gerald, 268.
    Dedicates 'Tiresias' to Fitz-Gerald, 285.
    Friendship of, with Fitz-Gerald, 66.
    His admiration of Fitz-Gerald's prose, 124.
Thackeray, W. M.—
    First met Fitz-Gerald at Cambridge, 13.
    Love of, for Fitz-Gerald, 220.
'The Meadows in Spring,' poem by Fitz-Gerald, 115.
Thompson, W. H., one of Fitz-Gerald's college friends, 13.
Trench, Archbishop, friendship of, with Fitz-Gerald, 324.
Tributes to Fitz-Gerald's genius by
    Asquith, H. H., 180.
    Clodd, Edward, 184.
    Hay, Colonel John, 177.

Index

Tributes to Fitz-Gerald's genius by
    M'Carthy, Justin Huntly, 183.
    Norton, Professor Charles Eliot, 175.
    Swinburne, Algernon Charles, 183.
    Williams, Dr. Talbot, 176.

WHERSTEAD LODGE, description of, 23.
Will, official copy of Fitz-Gerald's, 324.

Index

Tributes to FitzGerald's genius by:
McCarthy, Justin Huntly, 18
Norton, Professor Charles Eliot, 17
Swinburne, Algernon Charles, 18
Williams, Dr. Talbot, 170

Wrentmore Locke, inscription of, 17
A valuable copy of FitzGerald's, 170